The celebrated guide to healthful, economical,* gourmet fare from one of the world's great cuisines.

In addition to giving her marvelous recipes, Madame Grace Chu explains: the what-and-why of basic ingredients in Chinese cooking • how to cut with a Chinese cleaver • working with woks and chopsticks • the variety of cooking methods • the history of tea • the right way to order in a Chinese restaurant • how to grow bean sprouts in your own kitchen.

She also lists American stores where Chinese foods can be purchased, but she concentrates on ingredients easily purchased from your supermarket.

*Chinese food is low in cholesterol and uses small amounts of meat.

THE PLEASURES OF CHINESE COOKING
was originally published by
Simon and Schuster.

The Pleasures of
Chinese Cooking

by GRACE ZIA CHU

Illustrations by Grambs Miller

Foreword by Craig Claiborne

PUBLISHED BY POCKET BOOKS NEW YORK

THE PLEASURES OF CHINESE COOKING

Simon and Schuster edition published September, 1962

POCKET BOOK edition published March, 1969
2nd printing........................April, 1976

This POCKET BOOK edition includes every word contained in
the original, higher-priced edition. It is printed from brand-
new plates made from completely reset, clear, easy-to-read type.
POCKET BOOK editions are published by
POCKET BOOKS,
a division of Simon & Schuster, Inc.,
A GULF+WESTERN COMPANY
630 Fifth Avenue,
New York, N.Y. 10020.
Trademarks registered in the United States
and other countries.

ISBN: 0-671-80519-3.
Library of Congress Catalog Card Number: 62-15491.

Printed in the U.S.A.

This book is dedicated to
my teacher and friend—E. L. C.

My grateful thanks to all my friends and students for their interest, inspiration and suggestions, and to my two sons, Samuel and Daniel, for their encouragement and help in making this book a reality.

Contents

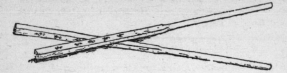

Menus Using Ingredients from Chinese Food Stores

Gourmet Dishes for Chinese Banquets   151

Chinese Hors d'Oeuvres   173

Four Regional Ways of Preparing Duck   205

Index   217

Foreword

Within the past decade in this country there has been a formidable surge of interest in Chinese cuisine. Primarily this interest has been reflected in the growth and popularity of Chinese restaurants, but it has also been marked in the American home.

There are many gastronomes, those who justly deserve the name without wearing it like a badge of honor, who believe that traditional Chinese cooking is among the most sophisticated on earth. It is infinitely more varied than French or Italian cuisine and, in essence, less complicated.

There is probably no one, certainly no one on the New York scene, who has done more to familiarize the public with the food of her homeland than Madame Grace Chu. The ability to cook well is an inborn talent, and Madame Chu, although high-born in an age when servants were a commonplace, is possessed of the magic involved in using the wok, the traditional cooking utensil, to the greater glory of the human palate. In person she has taught hundreds of New York men and women the joys of Chinese cuisine— and her book, simply written and easily understood, will enrich the table on a vaster scale.

Craig Claiborne
Food Editor, *The New York Times*

Part I

An Introduction
to Chinese Cooking

WE CHINESE LIKE TO THINK of cooking as a distinctive art form—and a very practical one at that. It is an art that should delight our senses. Or, as an old Chinese saying puts it, a well-prepared dish of food should appeal to the eye by its coloring; to the nose by its aroma; to the ear by its sounds (such as "crunch, crunch"); and, of course, to the mouth by its flavor.

The art of Chinese cooking was passed down from generation to generation, kept alive through word of mouth (mother telling daughter), through observation (watching the family chef in action), or simply through trial and error. Recipes were prized family secrets. The techniques of this art were developed and refined over thousands of years. Rare was the Chinese cook who bothered to set down his secrets in writing (Chinese cookbooks, such as this one, are a latter-day phenomenon).

For those who aspire to become professional Chinese chefs, the road can be long and difficult. Traditionally, the period of apprenticeship usually takes a minimum of three years, of which no less than two and a half years are spent just learning and practicing how to cut various foods properly. More often than not, the student chef is apt to find his teacher singularly uncooperative. The apprentice is never permitted to ask questions. Nor will an established

3

chef volunteer any information. Whatever the apprentice chef learns, he learns by watching his teacher at work. And three years of watching out of the corner of one's eye requires a certain amount of patience and perseverance.

The rewards of Chinese chefdom, however, can be great. If I may cite a personal experience, I'd like to tell of a particular party I attended while I was in Chungking, the capital of China during World War II. This banquet was to be prepared by the city's most famous chef, Ku Ku-yen. After all the guests had been seated around the table, I noticed that one chair had been left vacant—deliberately. It then dawned on me that the chair had been left for Chef Ku, as a sign of respect, even though our good chef probably hadn't the vaguest intention of joining our party.

Just as the host was raising the cup for the first toast, a scholarly-looking little man—Chef Ku himself—came shuffling in from the direction of the kitchen. He bowed and apologized profusely for not being able to join the party, since he was going to have his hands full in the kitchen. With this pronouncement, he disappeared from view once more, not to reappear until the very end of the party. Then he came shuffling in again to accept toasts offered in tribute to the chef and to his mastery of the cooking art.

This is not to suggest that anyone who attempts Chinese cooking can expect to hear cheers and hurrahs for the rest of his life But for Americans who want to learn Chinese cookery, there is this consolation: you won't have to spend three years in apprenticeship. In some large cities in the United States, special classes in Chinese cooking are offered in local educational institutions. Those who do not live in a city that offers these courses can learn the do-it-yourself way —with the help of a Chinese cookbook.

I have taught Chinese cooking for many years, both in my home and at the China Institute in America. These experiences have given me some insight as to the Chinese foods that Americans are most likely to enjoy. The availability of Chinese materials and ingredients in the United States has been kept in mind in planning the recipes in this book. And I can assure you that every recipe has been tested time and again, both by myself and by hundreds of my cooking students.

The book is organized along the general lines of my cooking courses: Part I introduces the reader to those ingredients, tools and techniques that give the Chinese cuisine its own distinct character; Part II, beginning with the simpler recipes, proceeds gradually toward those dishes that are a little more difficult, and finally, in keeping with the developing skills and understanding of the student cooks, toward authentic banquet fare. Since most Americans are introduced to Chinese foods by going to Chinese-American restaurants, the recipes begin, after a description of the most popular foods served in these restaurants, with directions for making these dishes.

Next is a group of menus for dishes calling for *only* those ingredients obtainable at American food stores, but prepared in the Chinese way. As students gain experience, they can move on to recipes that list special, but easily obtainable, Chinese ingredients, for more complicated, exotic Chinese gourmet dishes. Then there is a section on Chinese hors d'oeuvres for lunches, teas and cocktail parties. Finally, there are four regional ways to prepare duck.

Students who have taken my cooking courses often bombard me with questions: Must this dish be served as soon as it is prepared? What dessert should be served following Millionaire Chicken? When can I serve tea? Unlike Chinese chefs, I always try to answer these questions. In anticipation of the questions that you may have, I have included a number of *tips*—labeled as such—immediately following most of the recipes. These *tips* will let you know whether a particular dish can be prepared well before serving time, whether some ingredients can be substituted for others, and so on. To answer the big question of which dish goes with what, I have organized many of the recipes into groups of menus, rather than to present a hodgepodge of individual recipes. This, of course, need not stop you from trying any individual recipe by itself. Nor need you be afraid to combine your own menus, picking a dish from one section and a second from another.

This book will, I hope, lead you into many happy and successful experiences with Chinese cookery. The variety provided by Chinese cooking is virtually endless (the Chinese know over two hundred and fifty ways to cook pork alone!). Perhaps no other cooking in the world lends itself more to the individual talents and ingenuity of the cook. This is what makes Chinese cooking so rewarding. More than that, Chinese cooking is fun.

Ingredients:
The "What" of Chinese Cooking

PERHAPS THE FIRST THING any would-be Chinese cook learns is what the Chinese consider to be the basic ingredients of cooking. We Chinese say that to begin housekeeping there are seven *must* items: oil, salt, soy sauce, vinegar, fuel, rice and tea. Let's talk about each of these items individually.

Oil. The most widely used cooking oil in China is bean oil extracted from soybeans. Others include peanut oil, cabbage-seed oil, sesame-seed oil, cottonseed oil, lard, chicken fat, and sometimes even duck fat. For family cooking, peanut oil is the odds-on favorite because it is considered the "best tasting"—that is, it is least likely to disturb the taste of the food prepared with it. When preparing a banquet, however, most Chinese restaurants are apt to use lard. Whenever chicken fat is used in particular dishes, most restaurants will announce the fact in their menus. Butter is rarely used; there has always been a scarcity of dairy products in China and the majority of Chinese have never acquired a taste for it.

Salt. The common, ordinary variety of table salt is taken for granted by Americans because, well, it *is* so common and ordinary. Not so in China, where salt is often

7

a prized commodity. The Chinese obtain most of their salt through the evaporation of sea water. For the people living in China's interior provinces, thousands of miles from the coast, salt is often hard to come by. Because of inadequate transportation facilities, it is difficult and costly to carry salt to the inland regions. In the past, the taxes levied by local authorities on each shipment as it passed through their provinces so inflated the price of salt that most families could not afford it. This was the reason that, in certain regions of China, cooks took to using vinegar and hot peppers as salt substitutes to bring out flavor in food.

Soy sauce. The one ingredient that most characterizes Chinese cookery is a dark, salty liquid that goes under the name of soy sauce. All types of soy sauce are made from soybeans, water and salt, although the sauce comes in many grades and shades of color, from dark brown to darker brown to darkest brown. Various regions of China produce their own types of soy sauce, differing according to the techniques of the makers and the source and quality of the water used (just as in brewing beer, similar factors impart distinctive characteristics to the final produce). Ordinary soy sauce of a serviceable if undistinguished type can be bought at most American grocery stores today.

Vinegar. In Chinese cookery the most commonly used vinegar is that made from rice. Red wine vinegar, familar to most American cooks, most closely resembles Chinese vinegar in flavor and color and will serve as a suitable substitute.

Fuel. To American cooks commanding gleaming kitchens with gadget-bedecked gas or electric ranges, it may seem odd to list fuel as an ingredient of cooking. But to cooks in China, fuel has to be collected before cooking is possible at all. For longer than most people would care to remember, Chinese cooks have had to use wood, charcoal, coal, twigs, leaves—indeed, almost anything that can be gathered, dried and burned—as cooking fuel. Incidentally, the reason that a Chinese cook cuts his meats and vegetables into small pieces for cooking is to permit the food to cook faster. Less cooking time means less fuel consumed. Reduced fuel consumption obviously means less woodchopping, less coal digging, less twig picking.

Rice. The staple food of China, or, more accurately, of about two thirds of China, is rice. For the other third, primarily the northern and northwestern regions, the staple food is more likely to be wheat, beans, millet, barley or other grains (the Chinese sometimes use the word "rice" loosely to mean grain of all kinds). Long-grained rice is the best type to use for general cooking purposes, although for congee (a sort of porridge, usually served at breakfast time) short-grained rice is more suitable. Sweet rice, also known as glutinous rice, is used primarily in pastries and special festival dishes.

Tea. As what might be called the standard beverage of the Chinese, tea has a story that requires considerable telling. So I have saved this item for a separate section in another part of this book.

These basic seven are the most important ingredients in Chinese cooking, but, of course, one can hardly cook a palatable meal with these alone. Here are some of the other ingredients that help to lend a distinctive character to Chinese cookery.

Tea container, jasmine sprig and modern soy sauce bottle

Wines are sometimes required in the preparation of Chinese dishes, particularly those with seafood. As every experienced cook knows, seafood has a tendency to smell—yes, fishy. Chinese cooks long ago discovered that adding a dash of rice wine during the cooking of seafoods will mask this odor. Dry sherry is an adequate substitute for rice wine for cooking purposes. In most recipes just a teaspoonful or a tablespoonful of wine is all that is needed, except in such special dishes as "Drunk" Chicken, "Drunk" Pork and Peking Duck, where a stronger wine flavor is desired.

Sugar is often added to those recipes that require soy sauce in their preparation. Regular granulated sugar will serve for most purposes, although a few recipes may require brown sugar. The quantity of sugar added is usually very small.

Fresh ginger root appears most frequently in fish, seafood, meat and poultry dishes. Ginger roots may be obtained in Chinese food stores (some of these are listed on pages 39–40), in Greek and Spanish stores, and in American specialty-food stores. Only a few slices of fresh ginger root are required to create the desired taste-effect. Please note that dry ginger and ground ginger powder are *not* adequate substitutes for fresh ginger root. To store fresh ginger root, scrape the skin off each piece and then wash and dry the pieces. Put the ginger in a jar, add enough dry sherry to cover the ginger, and cap tightly. In cold weather it is perfectly all right to store ginger so prepared on an open shelf, although it is advisable to keep it in the refrigerator in warm weather. The ginger will keep indefinitely when properly stored.

Scallions, leeks, and *chives* are also added to certain dishes to enhance their taste. Both the white and the green parts of scallions, cut into varying lengths, are used.

Garlic is most used in the so-called northern-style Chinese cooking. It is usually sautéed in the frying pan before the meats and the vegetables are added. Should the garlic be removed from the pan prior to the addition of the other ingredients? Or should the garlic be left in the

Ginger root

Pewter wine pot and cups

pan to cook with the meats and vegetables? Either way. The choice is left to the discretion and taste of the individual cook.

Cornstarch is used primarily to thicken soups, sauces and gravies. It is also used to coat fish and meat to preserve their flavor and tenderness. Novice cooks sometimes use cornstarch to excess. Avoid overuse of cornstarch in any single dish.

Monosodium glutamate is the awesome name of a white-powdered condiment which, sold under such trade names as Ac'cent, has in recent years become a familiar item in American markets. This powder has been used by Chinese cooks for years and years—and years. In using monosodium glutamate, remember that a little goes a long way. A pinch of this powder will enhance virtually any dish, be it vegetable, soup, seafood, meat or poultry. But too much will give every dish you make the same taste—the taste of monosodium glutamate. The use of this flavoring powder is not essential, although, as a matter of personal preference, I like to add a little to most recipes.

Black pepper, hot red pepper and *Szechuen pepper* are the most frequently used of the spices. Szechuen pepper (xanthoxym, or, in Chinese, *hwa-chiao*) is a pepper that looks like the usual peppercorn; it is mildly hot and has a pleasant scent. *Star anise* is often used to add zest to certain dishes. Another popular spice goes under the collective name of *five-spice powder* and consists of anise seed, fennel, clove, cinnamon bark and *hwa-chiao*, ground into powder and mixed together.

Chinese parsley (or *hsiang-tsai*, which means "fragrant vegetables") looks like parsley, but isn't. It is actually fresh coriander, which Latin Americans call *culantro* or *cilantro*. Chinese parsley may be used to garnish a cold dish or, when chopped into fine bits, to mix into soups and chopped-meat dishes. Although it is used mostly to add a touch of color, there are gourmets who enjoy it for its flavor.

Water chestnut, as the name implies, is a type of vegetable grown in a flooded field; it is not to be confused with the chestnuts sold roasted on the street. When the bulb-like roots of the water chestnuts are fully matured, the field is drained. The water chestnuts continue to grow for a few more days and are then harvested. Freshly gathered water chestnuts are especially tasty and juicy. They may be eaten as fruits or sliced and added to various dishes for flavor and texture; or, when dried and ground into powder, used as a binding or thickener.

Bamboo shoots. Many varieties of bamboo shoots are grown in all parts of China. Each bamboo plant produces at least three crops of shoots during a calendar year. Depending on the time of harvest, the crop is known as spring bamboo, summer bamboo, or winter bamboo (as to what happened to autumn bamboo, your guess is as good

Water chestnut and Chinese parsley

Bamboo shoots and Chinese mushrooms

as mine). Of the three types, summer bamboo shoots are the tenderest, but most bamboo shoots canned in the Far East and shipped to foreign markets are of the winter variety.

Chinese mushrooms, dried, are used in many dishes, along with bamboo shoots and ham slices, to add color, texture and flavor. In color and shape, Chinese mushrooms resemble the dried mushrooms imported from Italy and central Europe, but the flavor of Chinese mushrooms is not so strong as that of their European cousins. Both fresh and dried mushrooms are used in Chinese cookery, but one should not be considered a substitute for the other.

Three other vegetables deserve a word of identification. *Snow peas* look like regular pods of green peas; but they are very special young, tender peas of which you eat the pods and all. *Bok choy* is a cabbage with white stems and green leaves, very popular in Chinese cooking. And *celery cabbage*, often called Chinese cabbage, is a long cabbage shaped like romaine lettuce, usually white but sometimes green. It is good in salad.

Hoisin sauce and *oyster sauce* are two Chinese sauces that bear mentioning. Hoisin sauce is a thick, dark sauce that might be considered a Chinese version of ketchup. Usually sold at Chinese groceries in cans, Hoisin sauce is used both in cooking and as a dip. Oyster sauce is made of oysters and brine. A dash of oyster sauce in place of soy sauce will add a unique flavor to certain meat and vegetable dishes.

Snow peas

Chinese celery cabbage

OYSTER SAUCE
OYSTERS YEAST
SOY BEANS

Bok choy

HOISIN SAUCE

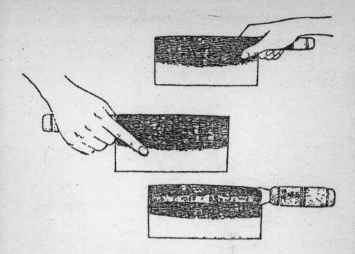

Cutting
with a Chinese Cleaver

ABOVE ALL OTHER KITCHEN UTENSILS, a Chinese cook tends to prize a set of razor-sharp cleavers. For example, many Chinese chefs have their own personal sets of cleavers which they guard zealously for fear that someone may misuse them and ruin their cutting edge. A chef would not think of lending his cleavers any more than a violinist would casually lend his favorite instrument.

The Chinese-style cleaver is a heavy knife with a broad and—believe it or not—rectangular-shaped blade. An unusually versatile utensil, the cleaver can be used to cut, slice, chop, shred, and even mince, all types of meat and vegetables. It is also useful in crushing garlic and ginger. Its broad blade can serve as a spatula for transporting the cut meats and vegetables from the cutting board to the pot or pan—but don't use the cleaver as a spatula during cooking, just as you would not use a cutting knife for this purpose.

As with any sharp instrument—and Chinese cleavers are sharp!—take care to avoid injury. When the Chinese

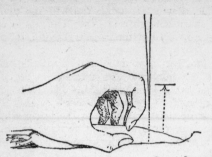

Straight cutting

cleaver is used properly, it is practically impossible to cut yourself with it.

Using the Chinese cleaver. Before you start cutting, make sure that your cutting board is set directly in front of you and that it will not slide around while you are working with the cleaver. Now hold the cleaver with your right hand (assuming that you are right-handed; if not, simply switch the right- and left-hand movements in the instructions that follow). The blade should fall across the cutting board at about a 45-degree angle; this is the most natural and comfortable working position, and besides, it's the best way to be able to see what you're doing.

Slide your right hand up the handle of the cleaver far enough so that your extended thumb and first finger fall naturally on the sides of the blade—the thumb on one side and the first finger on the other. Be sure to hold the cleaver firmly, but you need not clutch it in a life-or-death grip.

Your left hand holds onto the object to be cut. Curve the fingers of your left hand downward and inward until the first knuckle extends beyond the finger tips. The cleaver should be placed so that the side of the broad blade just touches the first knuckle; the knuckles now serve as a cutting guide.

The cutting motion itself is a forward and downward press—*not* a back-and-forth sawing motion. And never, never, never swing the cleaver like an ax. Remember, you are cutting food, not chopping wood. For safety's sake, never lift the cutting edge any higher than the level of the first knuckle of your left hand. You will find that a Chinese cleaver is sharp enough and heavy enough to cut through practically any food without your having to exert undue pressure.

As you progress in your cutting, gradually move the left hand back, leaving what still remains to be cut in place, still keeping the fingers curved and using the first knuckle as a cutting guide. This cutting technique may seem a little awkward at first. Do it slowly in the beginning; with just a little practice, you'll soon find yourself cutting away as deftly as a professional Chinese chef.

The different ways to cut. In Chinese cookery, cutting is not merely a matter of making little pieces from big pieces. There are many practical considerations which make cutting techniques an important aspect of cooking in the Chinese way.

For one thing, smaller pieces take less time to cook. For another, most Chinese recipes combine meat and vegetables in the same dish, and the sizes and shapes of the meat and vegetables must be similar to insure uniformity in appearance and in cooking time required. For example, if pork is used in a recipe that calls for the meat to be cut into shreds, then the vegetables—be they bamboo shoots or string beans or whatever—will also, in most cases, be cut into shreds, so that both the meat and the vegetable will be cooked in the same length of time. Another reason cutting is important is that the Chinese use chopsticks to pick up the food. Even experienced chopsticks users will tell you it is considerably easier to pick up a small piece of food than a large one with a pair of chopsticks. Finally, we Chinese cut our food into small pieces because—well, we just think it looks and tastes better that way. Here are some of the different methods of cutting used in Chinese cooking.

1. *Slicing:* There are two ways to slice—the straight slice and the slant slice. Let's say we are about to cut a carrot. In straight slicing, the carrot is placed perpendicular to the broad side of the cleaver. The thickness of the slices varies according to the individual recipe. For slant slicing, our victim (the carrot) should be placed at about a 45-degree angle to the broad side of the cleaver. Pieces

sliced in a slant will therefore be larger than those cut by straight slicing.

2. *Shredding:* This is probably the most common cutting method used in Chinese cooking, since it is most adaptable to *stir frying* (quick frying), a cooking technique used for many, many different Chinese dishes. In shredding, proceed as in slant slicing. After the carrot (using the carrot again merely as an example) is cut in slant slices, cut each slice further into very thin strips, or shreds.

3. *Dicing:* As its name implies, this is a method of cutting vegetables or meats into the shape of small dice, more or less. An easy way to do this is to cut the food lengthwise into half-inch strips. Then cut each strip into half-inch segments. The result should be lots of litttle die-shaped pieces.

4. *Oblique cutting:* Actually a fairly simple way to cut, oblique cutting sounds complicated because it is a little hard to explain in words. I'll give it a try anyway, and hope that the illustrations on page 19 will make the explanation clearer.

Using that carrot as an example for the last time, you make your first slice as if you were beginning to slant slice. But before you make the second slice, roll the carrot toward you with a quarter-turn. You'll know that you've made a quarter-turn if the cut you have just made is facing directly upward. Now give the carrot another slant slice, then another roll, another slice, another roll—and so on.

At first you may think that oblique cutting is a lot of foolishness. But, aha! there's a reason for it. Take a look at the carrot you have just cut. Notice that the cut carrot now has many exposed surfaces that will absorb flavor in cooking. In addition, oblique cutting breaks up the "strings" of fibrous vegetables. And, for further reasons that I won't even attempt to explain, vegetables cut obliquely are more tender than vegetables cut in other ways.

Oblique cutting is almost always used in those recipes where vegetables are cooked slowly with meats. In such

Slicing

Shredding

Dicing

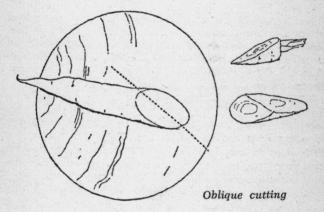

Oblique cutting

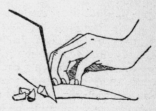

recipes the meats are usually cut in chunk style, rather than sliced, shredded or diced.

As I said earlier, the Chinese cleaver can be used to chop and to mince, as well as to cut and to slice; but I suggest that for these we take the easy way out. Mincing and chopping can both be done quicker with a hand or electric grinder—so why don't we just do it that way?

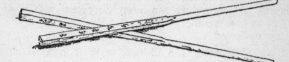

Working with Woks and Chopsticks

No CHINESE COOK would consider his kitchen equipment complete without woks and chopsticks, any more than without his set of cleavers. The *wok* (also known as *kuo-tse*) is the all-purpose cooking pan of the Chinese kitchen. As for chopsticks, a Chinese cook would hate to be caught without them. I hasten to add, however, that it isn't absolutely necessary to have either cleaver, wok or chopsticks in order to prepare Chinese food. Beginning students who don't happen to have these tools in their kitchens should not be discouraged from attempting to cook in the Chinese way. Obviously, a kitchen knife can take the place of a cleaver—although you might have a hard time convincing a Chinese chef of this—and a frying pan can substitute for a wok. And you don't *have* to eat with chopsticks.

I mention them for two reasons. First, I want to give the beginning student an idea of how the Chinese actually prepare their foods. Second, I hope that many American students of Chinese cooking will want eventually to have these utensils for their own kitchens. In my years of teaching Chinese cooking, I have found that many of my students grow strangely attached to them, once they have learned how to use them. Many have told me that they use the cleaver, the woks and the chopsticks not only when they get the urge to whip up a Chinese dish but in their everyday cooking as well. These tools are inexpensive and not so difficult to obtain as you might think. For those who may wish to have them, many of the Chinese stores listed on pages 39–40 stock utensils too. Here are brief descriptions of both wok and chopsticks and, more important, a few words on how to use them.

The *wok* is a Chinese cooking pan which resembles a salad bowl on which someone has thoughtfully tacked a pair of handles. Woks come in various sizes and are usually made of iron, aluminum or copper. The Chinese cook uses his woks for everything from stir frying to braising to stewing to deep frying. Woks are easily adapted to cooking for one person or six, eight or ten.

A Chinese kitchen ordinarily has a minimum of two woks: a large one for cooking rice and a smaller one for preparing meats and vegetables by frying, braising or stewing. Bamboo steamers of one or two sections may be fitted over the large wok to steam or warm up other foods during the rice-cooking process, while the meat and vegetables cook in the smaller wok. Hence it is possible to prepare a multi-course meal with the use of only two woks.

The first wok-maker (whose name, alas, has long since been lost to history) designed the round-bottomed wok to fit Chinese stoves, which burn wood, hay, coal or charcoal. Naturally he had no idea that persons would come along later—much later—to invent the gas range and electric stove with their flat-topped burning units. The round-bottomed wok does not sit very steadily on a modern cooking range. For this reason, someone came along and designed a metal ring, its sides perforated with air holes, to hold the wok steadily on a gas or electric range so that it will not tip over while you are using it. When buying a wok, be sure to buy one of these ring-shaped wok-holders as well.

Wok on ring

The wok must be seasoned before using to prevent food from sticking to it. After buying a new wok, wash it with hot water and soap, then grease the entire inside surface with vegetable oil. Heat the wok over a high flame on the ring for a minute, then rinse with hot water. Repeat the process. Wash the wok carefully, and only with hot water. The wok is now ready to use. The shape of the wok makes it very easy to clean, as it has no corners in which food can stick. After the wok has been seasoned, it should not again be washed with detergent or soap. Instead, scrape it clean with a stiff brush and rinse in very hot water. If your wok is made of iron—most are—be sure, after rinsing, to dry immediately over a flame for a few seconds to prevent rusting.

Chopsticks not only serve as eating utensils but also are useful in the kitchen for stirring, mixing, whipping and sorting. They are made in varying shapes and sizes and from various materials. There are chopsticks made of gold and silver, of ivory, coral, wood, bamboo and, yes, even twentieth-century plastics. There are long chopsticks (about 20 inches) and short ones (5 inches), round and angled ones. Which kind should you use? It's a matter of personal preference, except that for actual cooking you must use *only* chopsticks made of wood or bamboo. Metal chopsticks conduct heat too well, ivory ones will turn yellow with heat, and plastic ones may melt away.

Using chopsticks. Some things are easier said than done, as any beginner manipulating a pair of chopsticks for the first time can tell you. To the uninitiated, working a pair of chopsticks may seem like the ultimate in finger exercises. But it's not that hard—really! A sizable part of the world's population eats with them every day. All it takes to master their use is a little practice and a little persistence.

Start by grasping the chopsticks about two-thirds of the way up from the lower tips (the smaller ends). The tips of the two chopsticks should meet. If they don't, you are in for trouble. Push up on the two tips until they are even. Now, here's a finger-by-finger account on how to work the chopsticks. Remember, one will remain stationary as the other one moves.

The stationary chopstick should be cradled at the angle

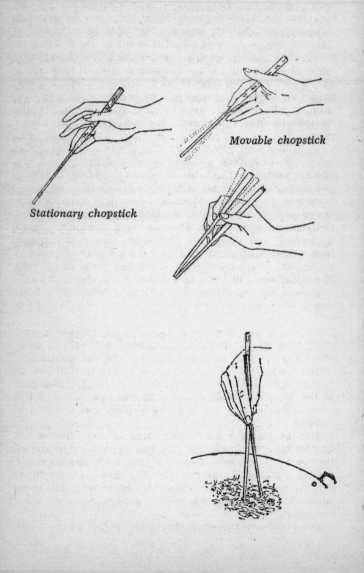

Movable chopstick

Stationary chopstick

of your thumb and index finger (you don't have to pinch the chopstick, but hold it firmly enough so that it won't slip). Next, rest the other end on the tips of your ring finger and little finger and bend them so that the tips are even. At this point, half the battle is won. You have just secured the stationary chopstick in its proper position. It wasn't so hard, was it?

Now we come to the movable chopstick. Place this chopstick so that the shaft runs between the thumb and the index finger, near the tips of both fingers. Curve your middle finger below this chopstick so that the shaft rests on the tips of both fingers. At the point where your thumb cuts across both shafts, the chopsticks should be an inch apart.

By flexing your index and middle fingers, you should be able to bring the tip of the movable chopstick to meet the tip of the stationary one. It is between these two tips that the food is grasped. Try it. All tangled up? Start over and try it again. At first, don't hesitate to use your free hand to help you move the chopsticks into position. After a while you'll be able to do it as a one-handed operation. You may also find it difficult at first to get the tip of one chopstick to come to terms with the tip of the other. That, too, will come with practice.

Methods:
The "How" of Chinese Cooking

THE SEEMINGLY ENDLESS VARIETIES of cooking methods employed by the Chinese chef are limited only by his imagination and the equipment he has on hand. One little used and somewhat primitive way of baking chicken, for example, is simply to encase the fowl in wet mud and bury it in a fire—an ingenious if messy way to cook.

Fortunately the Chinese have devised other and more appealing cooking methods. Among the techniques that are frequently used in cooking Chinese dishes at home are stir frying, shallow frying, deep frying, clear simmering, red stewing, braising and steaming.

Stir frying. Just as its name implies, this is a technique of frying foods over a high flame, stirring continuously meanwhile. A small amount of cooking oil is used —only enough to cover the bottom of the frying pan. The oil is placed in the pan to heat before the other ingredients are added. The food should be stirred vigorously and continuously for the duration of the cooking, which is usually only a few minutes. If the food seems dry and tends to stick to the wok or frying pan, a little water may be added.

Because in stir frying the cooking time is relatively brief, dishes to be stir fried should be prepared last, when there are other foods to be prepared by slower cooking methods, so that everything will be ready for the table at the same time. Stir-fried dishes are at their best when served piping hot.

If a comparison must be drawn, stir frying can be said to resemble sautéeing. Stir frying is the most common method of cooking Chinese food.

Shallow frying. This technique differs from stir frying in that a medium flame is used and a longer cooking period is required. There is no need to stir the food during cooking. Using just enough cooking oil to cover the bottom of the frying pan, the food is spread evenly in the pan and allowed to fry slowly for a few minutes. The food may then be turned once or twice. When it takes on a brownish color, it is done. This method is usually used for food which has been presteamed, prefried or preboiled.

Deep frying. This method should be familiar to anyone who has ever tried to make French-fried potatoes; the technique is exactly the same. Heat at least a cup of vegetable oil to about 375 degrees. Test temperature with an oil thermometer. Drop the food gently into the oil. The cooking time depends on the type, size and density of the food being fried. The food is ready when it turns a golden brown.

Clear simmering. A method for making soups, clear simmering is so called because the food is cooked in water—just plain water. Meats and vegetables are simmered in water for a relatively long period of time, usually from two to four hours. A dash of salt may be added just before completion. When ingredients are strained off, this technique produces a very clear soup with all the natural flavor of the meats and vegetables.

Red stewing. A uniquely Chinese style of cooking, red stewing is similar to clear simmering, except that the food is cooked in soy sauce and water rather than water alone, the soy sauce giving the food its reddish-brown coloring. Sherry, ginger and scallions are often added to red-stewed dishes. In red stewing, the pot is brought to a boil over a high flame; the flame is progressively reduced to medium, then low. Cooking time is similar to that required for clear simmering. One advantage of this type of cooking is that leftovers can be warmed and rewarmed for future use. Some claim that the flavor of the food improves with rewarming.

This may be a good place to point out that we Chinese do *not* use soy sauce in the cooking of every dish. Because soy sauce darkens food, it is never used in those dishes where the natural color of the food is to be retained. In red stewing, however, soy sauce is always used.

Braising. Chinese cooks often use this technique for cooking meats. The first part of the method is similar to stir frying, but with less stirring. After the meat is well seared on all sides, other ingredients are added according to the individual recipe. Mix thoroughly and then proceed as in red stewing.

Steaming. The Chinese use a multi-layered pan for steaming. For those who have never seen one of these steam pots, the setup looks like several individual pots piled one on top of the other. The pot on the bottom is simply a large saucepan, where water is boiled to create steam. Each of the pots above the base saucepan has a perforated bottom, so that the steam created in the bottom pan will flow up and through to the top layer. As many layers are used as there are different foods to be cooked.

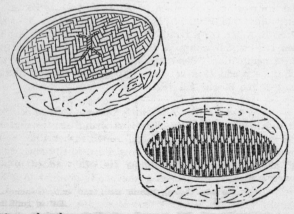

Chinese bamboo steamer

To a Chinese cook, the advantage of steaming is that several different dishes can be cooked at the same time, thereby saving fuel.

One thing should be remembered about steamed foods: While it is all right to reheat leftover steamed meats for use at another time, steamed fish and seafoods should not be reheated as a rule, as they become tough and lose their flavor. As far as these are concerned, what is not eaten the first time around will probably have to be thrown out.

If you do not have a steamer (please note that a double boiler is not a substitute), it is possible to set up a makeshift steamer that will serve adequately. The object is to keep the food high enough above the boiling water so that the water does not come in contact with the food—or else the food will be boiled. The steamer should have a lid snug enough to slow the escape of the steam, but not so tight that the pressure will build to a dangerous point. One such steamer, using common kitchen utensils, is illustrated in the diagram below.

Makeshift steamer, plate resting on tin can with top and bottom removed

The Story of Tea

MANY CENTURIES AGO, according to an old legend, a Chinese scholar was boiling water in the forest. By accident some leaves fell into the pot. The leaves made the water fragrant. When he drank it, he found that the water tasted bitter, yet there was a delicate and sweet after-taste which delighted him. Without realizing it the scholar had brewed and drunk the world's first pot of tea.

This is only one of the many legends on the origin of tea drinking. Few historians would vouch for the truth of such legends. But most experts on tea agree that tea drinking did originate in China. Historical writings reveal that the tea plant was cultivated there as early as the fourth century B.C. At first, tea was drunk for medicinal purposes—as a cure for lethargy as well as for all sorts of aches and pain.

By the sixth century A.D., the Chinese began to regard tea as a refreshing beverage. Poets were inspired by it; philosophers delved into deep thoughts while lingering over a cup of tea. The famous *Ch'a Ching* (Tea Classic) by Lu Yu was written in the time of the Tang Dynasty (A.D. 780). For his learned discourse on the various aspects of tea drinking, Lu Yu is honored by the Chinese as the patron saint of tea.

In the following centuries the cultivation of tea was introduced in India, Japan, Ceylon, Sumatra and Java. And European merchants, engaged in the Orient trade, shipped back cargoes of tea to their homelands—and touched off a lively controversy. Some Europeans denounced tea drinking; others defended and praised the practice. The second group prevailed. In time, tea was to become one of the most fashionable beverages in England and on the Continent.

Colonists brought tea with them to the New World. The ladies of New Amsterdam, it was reported, flavored their tea with peach leaves and nibbled lumps of sugar as they sipped. New Englanders, too, were fond of tea, but far less enthusiastic about the tea tax levied by the Government. This tax caused certain citizens of Boston to hold what was probably the most boisterous tea party in history.

Today, tea drinking is growing in popularity. Tea has been called one of the world's three great beverages—the others are cocoa and coffee. And, like almost everything else, the more that one knows about tea, the more enjoyable tea drinking can be.

The word "tea" comes from the Chinese (Amoy dialect) word *t'e*, pronounced something like "tay." Dutch traders brought this word to Europe; the English word "tea" is derived from it. Throughout most of China, the beverage is called *Ch'a*. Variations of the latter form are used in Japan, India, Persia and Russia.

The evolution of tea has passed through three main stages. First came the boiled tea in vogue during the time of the Tang Dynasty (eighth century). The tea leaves were pressed into hard bricks or cakes. To make tea, a chunk was broken off the tea brick and boiled in water. This way of making tea is rarely seen in China today, but is still quite common in Mongolia and some parts of Russia.

The next stage in the evolution of tea was whipped tea, developed during the Sung Dynasty (twelfth century). Using powdered tea leaves, a cup of tea was made by whipping (actually, just stirring with a whisk) the powder in hot water. This whipped tea might be considered the grandfather (perhaps great-great-great-etc.-grandfather) of the "instant tea" of today.

The third stage of tea's evolution was (and is) steeped tea. This is the most common way of making tea today. Every time you drop tea leaves into a pot or pop a tea bag into a cup and then add boiling water, you are making steeped tea.

The tea plant growing wild can reach a height close to thirty feet. When the plant is under cultivation, it is more practical to limit its height to three to five feet. Water supply, climate, altitude and the time of the year during which the tea leaves are picked directly affect the flavor of the tea. Several varieties of tea may all come from the same plant; they become individual types through different processes of fermentation and curing.

The best tea is produced in a warm, damp climate. Unfermented tea is roasted directly after picking, while the fermented tea is left to stand in the muggy air.

There are over 250 kinds of Chinese tea. In general, they can all be classified under three main groupings: (1) Unfermented green tea with its natural bouquet and light color; (2) Fermented black tea, which, as might be expected, is darker in color; (3) Semi-fermented oolong tea, which combines the bouquet of green tea with the color of black tea. The scented teas, such as Jasmine tea, are made mostly from semi-fermented tea, while the smoky teas, such as Lapsang Souchong, are made from fermented tea.

It is a traditional Chinese custom to serve tea to guests who are visiting the home at any time of the day. As a form of courtesy, the tea leaves must be placed in individual cups and the tea brewed right in the cup. Each cup has a lid for this purpose. (This provides "proof" to the guests that the tea is freshly made and not something that has been sitting around in a pot for two or three days.) The cup may be refilled with boiling water two or three times, since the drinker knows that the second cup of tea is equal to or even better than the first cup.

It is important to know how to brew Chinese tea correctly. Fresh water must be used each time tea is to be made. While waiting for the water to boil, place half a teaspoon of tea in each cup. Then pour about one tablespoon of boiling water over the tea leaves. Cover the cup for one minute, then fill the cup with boiling water and serve. The same cup should be refilled at least once to get the full benefit of good Chinese tea.

What about sugar and cream? Chinese tea drinkers generally frown on such practices. But adding sugar or cream, or both, to tea need not be considered an unforgivable sin. The important thing is that tea drinking should provide relaxation and enjoyment to the fullest, regardless of form, type or brand of tea used.

Here is a list of some of the most familiar names of the different kinds of tea in China.

1. Unfermented tea, known as *green* tea:

Dragon Well green tea, the most famous of all green teas, grown in Chekiang province near a famous spring called the Dragon Well
Gunpowder, a green tea from north China
Lu An, a green tea from Anhwei province in east China
Water Nymph, a green tea from Kwantung province in south China

2. Semi-fermented tea, known as *oolong* tea:

Lo Cha, from Formosa
Oolong, from Formosa

3. Fermented tea, known as *black* tea:

Black Dragon, from Kwantung province
Iron Goddess of Mercy, from Fukien province
Keemun, most famous of black teas, from Anhwei province
Pu-erh, from Yünnan province

4. Scented tea:

Chrysanthemum tea, green tea with white aster
Jasmine tea, oolong tea with jasmine, from Fukien province and Formosa
Lichee tea, black tea with lichee flavoring
Rose tea, black tea with dried rosebuds
Water Nymph tea, green tea with narcissus

5. Smoky tea:

Lapsang Souchong, smoked black tea from Hunan province in central China

The Right Way to Order
in a Chinese Restaurant

THE STYLE OF ORDERING in an American restaurant might be described as "every man for himself." Each person orders his own main course as well as vegetables, salad, dessert and beverage. No two persons eat the same foods unless they want to.

Ordering in a Chinese restaurant is quite the opposite. There is no single main course, but a combination of main courses to be shared by everyone. The only food that you will have all to yourself is your own private bowl of rice.

A general rule to follow is to select as many dishes as there are people in your party. In choosing these, always strive for variety—in foods, ways of cooking and ways of cutting. For example, a varied selection might include meats in chunks, prepared in the so-called red-stewed way; a diced

34

seafood dish cooked in its natural juices; vegetables prepared by stir frying; and a cold dish of some sort. The combination should always be tasty, colorful and balanced in terms of nutritional values.

Since most of the Chinese restaurants in the United States follow the Cantonese style of cooking, let's select a dinner for four persons from a typical Cantonese restaurant menu. This dinner might include:

> *Egg Drop Soup*
> *Barbecued Spareribs*
> *Moo Goo Gai Pien*
> *Lobster Cantonese*
> *Plus rice, tea and dessert*

If there are six persons in this party, you might add two more dishes, such as:

> *Sweet-Sour Pork*
> *Flank Steak with Oyster Sauce*

Notice how this selection includes beef, pork, chicken, lobster and other assorted foods. This menu provides variety, and there will be enough for all to share.

If your party is ordering chop suey and chow mein, you can still apply the same rules. Again, for a party of four, you might select:

> *Beef Chop Suey*
> *Chicken Chow Mein*
> *Shrimp Egg Fu Yung*
> *Ham Fried Rice*

Of course, the easiest way to order in a Chinese restaurant is to shift the whole load on the captain or the head waiter. Give him your most pitiful look (a bit like a cocker spaniel at feeding time) and tell him that you implicitly trust his vast knowledge of Chinese foods. Also be sure to tell him in advance how much money you are prepared to invest in the meal. Then sit back and relax. More often than not, the head waiter will be pleased to suggest a selection for you, and more than likely you will be pleased by his selection.

Whether you want to choose your own meal or have it chosen for you, there are some key words in any Chinese menu that will help you to know what you are getting. Let's take Moo Goo Gai Pien. *Moo goo* mean mushrooms; *gai* means chicken; *pien* means sliced. Put them together and you have sliced chicken with mushrooms. Simple, isn't it?

Here are some other key words to watch for on a Chinese menu:

Bok choy: Chinese green cabbage

Bok opp: Squab

Char shue: Roast pork

Ding: Diced

Dong goo: Chinese mushrooms

Dow see: Fermented black beans

Gee yook: Pork

Guy choy: Chinese mustard greens

Guy lan: Broccoli

Har: Shrimps

How yow: Oyster sauce

Kew: Chunks

Loong har: Lobster

Ngar choy: Bean sprouts

Ngow yook: Beef

Opp: Duck

See: Shredded

Soong: Minced

Sub gum: Mixture of meats or vegetables

Yu: Fish

Growing Bean Sprouts
in Your Own Kitchen

TWO TYPES OF BEAN SPROUTS are used in Chinese cooking: mung bean sprouts and soybean sprouts. The more familiar type is the mung bean sprout (served in most Chinese-American restaurants), although we Chinese tend to favor the soybean variety.

Both are grown the same way, but it takes twice as long to grow soybean sprouts as it does mung bean sprouts—approximately six days for the soybeans and three days for the mung beans. You can actually grow either of these right in your own kitchen without too much difficulty.

Suppose you have decided, just for the fun of it, to grow and harvest your own crop of mung bean sprouts. First you will have to obtain dried mung beans (which look somewhat like dried peas—green like these, but smaller) from a Chinese food store (see pages 39–40 for partial listing). These beans are inexpensive and will keep for months when stored in a jar.

Wash four tablespoons of beans three or four times. Then soak the beans overnight in a cup of lukewarm water. The next day rinse again until the water is clear. Next, take a flat pan, with holes in the bottom for draining the water from the pan, and spread two layers of cheesecloth evenly across the bottom of the pan. If you don't have such a pan, use any old flat-bottomed pan and punch the holes yourself.

Now, spread the mung beans over the cheesecloth, sprinkle with a quarter of a cup of lukewarm water, then cover with a clean, wet cloth. Be sure to keep your private bean-sprout garden in a *dark* place, such as an oven, a closet or a basement, if you have one—so that your sprouts will be crunchy, tender and white. The place does not have to be pitch black, but the bean sprouts should *never* be in direct sunlight.

During the day only—there's no night work involved in growing sprouts—sprinkle your little garden once every four hours with a half-cup of water. In about three days' time your sprouts should be two inches long and ready for the cooking pan.

As mung beans produce seven times their volume of sprouts (one pound of dried mung beans will grow seven pounds of sprouts), be sure to use, for your first attempt, not more than four tablespoons of dried mung beans. You are sure to be delighted by your home-harvested crop of fresh, tender sprouts.

Stores Where
Chinese Foods Can Be Purchased

Eastern Trading Company*
2801 Broadway
New York 25, New York

Mon Kuo Company
51 Bayard Street
New York 13, New York

Mon Fong Wo Company
36 Pell Street
New York 13, New York

Wo Fat Company
16 Bowery
New York 13, New York

Yuit Hing Market
    Corporation*
23 Pell Street
New York 13, New York

Boston

Chong Lung
18 Hudson
Boston 11, Massachusetts

T. H. Lung
9 Hudson
Boston 11, Massachusetts

Quong Sun Wah Company
54 Beach Street
Boston 11, Massachusetts

Sun Sun
34 Oxford Street
Boston 11, Massachusetts

* Indicates that they will fill mail orders.

Chicago

Sung Chong Lung
2220 South Wentworth
  Avenue
Chicago 16, Illinois

Man Sing Wing Company
2229 South Wentworth
  Avenue
Chicago 16, Illinois

Quong Yick & Company
238 West 23rd Street
Chicago, Illinois

Los Angeles

Yee Sing Chong Company
960 North Hill Street
Los Angeles 12, California

Sam Ward Company
959 North Hill Street
Los Angeles 12, California

Kwong Dack Wo Company
702 North Spring Street
Los Angeles, California

Kwong On Lung
686 North Spring Street
Los Angeles, California

San Francisco

Gim Fat Company Inc.
953 Grant Avenue
San Francisco, California

Moon John
803 Grant Avenue
San Francisco 8, California

Quong Lee & Company
848 Grant Avenue
San Francisco 8, California

Wing Sing Chong Company*
1076 Stockton Street
San Francisco, California

Washington, D. C.

Mee Wah Lung Company
608 H. Street, N. W.
Washington, D. C.

New China Supply Company
709 H. Street, N. W.
Washington, D. C.

Tuck Cheong & Company*
617 H. Street, N. W.
Washington, D. C.

---

* Indicates that they will fill mail orders.

Part II

1. *POPULAR DISHES IN CHINESE-AMERICAN RESTAURANTS*

   THIS BUSINESS OF CHOP SUEY
      AND CHOW MEIN

   BEEF CHOP SUEY

   CHICKEN CHOW MEIN

   SHRIMP EGG FU YUNG

   HAM FRIED RICE

   WONTON SOUP

   EGG DROP SOUP

   GROUND STEAK WITH PEAS

   MOO GOO GAI PIEN

   BARBECUED SPARERIBS

   SHRIMP EGG ROLLS

This Business
of Chop Suey and Chow Mein

FOR THOSE OF YOU who have long wondered what chop suey and chow mein are all about, it may be comforting to know that you have plenty of company. Many Chinese, too, have been baffled by these two concoctions with the Chinese-sounding names. On my last visit to Shanghai after World War II, I was riding along a main thoroughfare when I spotted a neon sign that proclaimed to the world: GENUINE AMERICAN CHOP SUEY SERVED HERE. To the proprietor of that Shanghai restaurant, at least, chop suey was as American as turkey and cranberry sauce.

Is chop suey a Chinese dish? The best answer seems to be: more or less. Webster's dictionary makes a valiant attempt at defining chop suey as "a mélange served in Chinese restaurants, consisting typically of bean sprouts, onions, mushrooms, etc., and sliced meats fried and flavored with sesame oil." In its usual wisdom, the dictionary neatly sidesteps the issue of whether chop suey is a genuine product of China.

But it is generally conceded by people who worry about such things that chop suey was indeed invented by the Chinese—the Chinese who had migrated to America. The story of chop suey's origin has as many versions as there are ingredients in the mélange. Most versions attribute the invention of chop suey to the Chinese who came to this

44

country during the last century to work on the transcontinental railroads. Their employment, of course, lasted only as long as there were railroads to be built. Therefore, many of the Chinese laborers turned to other ways of making a living. Some turned to the washing-and-ironing business, and thereby gave rise to the ubiquitous Chinese hand laundries that are now a part of the American scene. Others reasoned, with indisputable logic, that people must eat. Thus the Chinese restaurant came to be.

At first the patrons of the Chinese restaurants were exclusively Chinese. True, the food served in these establishments was a bit strange, not at all what these Chinese were used to in their native land. The ingredients were different, for many of the Chinese delicacies were simply not available. Nevertheless, if chop suey wasn't exactly the real thing, it was at least a reasonable facsimile thereof.

One day, so the stories go, a group of Americans (they were either miners or prospectors or cowboys, depending on which version of the story you choose) wandered into a Chinese restaurant. They tried, and were delighted by, those new Chinese dishes called "chop suey." They might have been somewhat less delighted had they known that they had been eating "miscellaneous odds and ends," which is what the words chop suey mean in the Cantonese dialect. In any case, the American discoverers of chop suey soon spread the word, and the dish became firmly established in the New World. The evolution of chop suey was to go on over a span of years. After considerable experimentation, a number of "standard" chop suey dishes won their honored places on Chinese restaurant menus, where they remain now and, perhaps, forever.

Chow mein, chop suey's faithful partner, has a slightly different background. Chow mein (which simply means "fried noodles") has the distinction of being a genuine Chinese dish. The people of different sections of China have various ways of frying noodles. Unfortunately, the type of chow mein served in most Chinese restaurants in America —with noodles that are deep-fried and crisp, bearing some resemblance to certain breakfast foods—is not the chow mein of China. Yet, there are those who love it—and they are certainly welcome to enjoy chow mein in any form or shape.

Today, prepared chop suey and chow mein are available in virtually all food stores and supermarkets. They are usually precooked and come in jars, cans or frozen packages. On the whole they are inexpensive and no more difficult to prepare than, say, heating up a can of spaghetti. But there are certain advantages to preparing chop suey and chow mein from scratch. For one thing, do-it-yourself chop suey and chow mein are even less expensive than the pre-prepared kind. For another, your own versions usually taste better because they retain some of the flavors that are inevitably lost in the packaging process.

On the following pages, I have included one typical chop suey dish and a chow mein dish. You will also find recipes for other popular dishes that are frequently ordered by patrons in Chinese-American restaurants. The recipes are not difficult to follow, and they introduce you to the basic methods of preparing Chinese foods. The knowledge of how chop suey and chow mein are prepared, and what ingredients go into them, will make Chinese foods more fun, the next time you order them in a Chinese restaurant or serve them at home.

May I suggest to beginners using the recipes in this book that they be sure to read through the entire recipe, including Tips, before beginning to cook.

● BEEF CHOP SUEY

4 SERVINGS

INGREDIENTS

1 *pound sirloin tip*
½ *cup fresh or canned bean sprouts*
½ *cup fresh mushrooms, sliced*
¼ *cup carrot slices 2″ x ½″ x ¼″*
¼ *cup celery slices 2″ x ½″ x ¼″*
¼ *cup onion slices 2″ x ½″ x ¼″*
1 *tomato*
2 *tablespoons peanut or corn oil*
2 *tablespoons soy sauce*
1 *tablespoon dry sherry*
1 *teaspoon sugar*
½ *teaspoon salt*
¼ *teaspoon monosodium glutamate*
1 *tablespoon cornstarch*

PREPARATION

Marinate the whole piece of steak in 1 tablespoon dry sherry and 1 tablespoon soy sauce for 10 minutes. Broil till medium rare. Cool. Cut into slices 2″ x ½″ x ¼″.

Wash and drain the bean sprouts.

Wash and slice the fresh mushrooms.

Cut the tomato into 6-8 wedges.

Dissolve 1 tablespoon cornstarch in 2 tablespoons cold water.

COOKING PROCEDURES

Heat 2 tablespoons of oil in a frying pan over high flame and add onions, celery, carrots and mushrooms. Stir over fire until oil coats all the vegetables, about 2 minutes.

Still over high flame, add the remaining tablespoon soy sauce, 1 teaspoon sugar, ½ teaspoon salt and ¼ teaspoon monosodium glutamate. Mix again.

Add 2 tablespoons water, turn heat to medium, cover and cook for 2 minutes.

Mix in the bean sprouts and the steak slices. Stir.

Gradually add the dissolved cornstarch; stir until it thickens.

Add the tomato wedges; mix well. Cook for 1 more minute. Remove from flame and serve.

TIPS

This is a basic chop suey dish. If steak is omitted, it becomes an excellent vegetable chop suey. This dish can be varied by using cooked shrimps, veal, ham, turkey or chicken in place of beef.

Fresh bean sprouts are preferred, but if they are not available, canned sprouts may be used. Open the can the day before, or at least several hours before using. Drain off the liquid, rinse sprouts under cold water faucet for a few minutes and soak in cold water. This will restore the "crunchiness" to a certain extent and make the bean sprouts taste much sweeter.

If fresh mushrooms are not available, canned sliced mushrooms may be used. Substitute the juice of the canned mushrooms for the 2 tablespoons of water called for under *Cooking Procedures*. It will taste even better.

● *CHICKEN CHOW MEIN*
4 SERVINGS

INGREDIENTS

8 *ounces thin spaghetti*
1 *cup cooked chicken, shredded*
½ *cup fresh or canned bean sprouts*
    (*see* Tips, *above*)
½ *cup shredded celery*
½ *cup shredded Chinese cabbage*
2 *tablespoons peanut or corn oil*
2 *tablespoons soy sauce*
1 *teaspoon sugar*
1 *tablespoon cornstarch*
¼ *teaspoon monosodium glutamate*
½ *cup clear chicken broth*

PREPARATION

Drop spaghetti in 2 quarts of boiling water and boil for 3 minutes. Drain.

Steam the spaghetti in a colander or steamer for 20 minutes. It will not stick together. Deep fry in hot oil until crisp.

Dissolve 1 tablespoon cornstarch in 2 tablespoons water.

COOKING PROCEDURES

Heat 2 tablespoons oil in a frying pan over high flame and sauté the Chinese cabbage and celery for about 2 minutes.

Add 2 tablespoons soy sauce, 1 teaspoon sugar and ¼ teaspoon monosodium glutamate. Mix well.

Add ½ cup chicken broth and bring to boil.

Add bean sprouts and shredded chicken and mix.

When it begins to boil, thicken with cornstarch.

Place fried spaghetti on a large platter and pour the mixture over it. Serve hot.

TIPS

Chow mein has become so popular that pre-fried noodles are now available in many food stores. These pre-prepared noodles save time and effort. But if you like to start from scratch, thin spaghetti is the nearest thing to Chinese noodles.

Cooked beef, shrimps and other ingredients may be used in place of chicken to make Beef Chow Mein, Shrimp Chow Mein, etc.

● *SHRIMP EGG FU YUNG*
4 SERVINGS

INGREDIENTS

4 *eggs*
½ *cup cooked shrimps*
1 *cup fresh or canned bean sprouts*
  (*see Tips, page 48*)
¼ *cup chopped onions*
¼ *cup chopped fresh mushrooms*
1 *scallion, chopped*
1 *tablespoon soy sauce*
1 *teaspoon salt*
½ *teaspoon sugar*
4 *tablespoons peanut or corn oil*

INGREDIENTS FOR SAUCE:
½ *cup clear chicken broth*
1 *teaspoon soy sauce*
½ *teaspoon salt*
¼ *teaspoon monosodium glutamate*
2 *teaspoons cornstarch*

PREPARATION

Beat the 4 eggs thoroughly.

Cut the shrimps into small pieces.

With 1 tablespoon oil, sauté the onions, mushrooms and scallion for 1 minute. Add bean sprouts and shrimps. Then add 1 tablespoon soy sauce, 1 teaspoon salt and ½ teaspoon sugar. Mix well. Place in dish and let cool.

Combine beaten eggs with cooled cooked mixture.

COOKING PROCEDURES

Using a frying pan 4″ in diameter, heat 2 teaspoons oil over low flame. When oil is hot, ladle in about ¼ the egg mixture. Cook until eggs have browned on one side. Turn over and brown the other side. Place in dish and set aside. Repeat this process, adding oil as necessary, until eggs are used up.

Pour sauce over pancakes and serve hot. Makes 4-5 pancakes.

COOKING PROCEDURES FOR SAUCE

Bring to boil ½ cup chicken broth and add 1 teaspoon soy sauce, ½ teaspoon salt and ¼ teaspoon monosodium glutamate. Dissolve 2 teaspoons cornstarch in 1 tablespoon cold water and gradually stir into the sauce until it thickens.

TIPS

The egg portion of this recipe can be prepared early in the day and reheated later in a double boiler or in the oven. The sauce, however, should be made just before serving to get best results.

Shreds of roast pork, roast beef, chicken or turkey can all be substituted for the shrimps.

- *HAM FRIED RICE*
  4 SERVINGS

INGREDIENTS

> 4 *cups cold boiled rice*
> 2 *eggs*
> ½ *cup diced cooked ham*
> ¼ *cup scallions cut into* ¼″ *pieces*
> 2 *tablespoons soy sauce*
> ½ *teaspoon sugar*
> ¼ *teaspoon monosodium glutamate*
> 4 *tablespoons peanut or corn oil*

PREPARATION

Beat the eggs and scramble them slightly (without adding milk or water) in 1 tablespoon of oil. Set aside for later use.

COOKING PROCEDURES

In a heavy frying pan over a high flame heat 3 tablespoons oil. Add scallions and stir a few times.

Add rice and stir quickly so that rice will not stick to the pan and will be well coated with the oil.

Add 2 tablespoons soy sauce, ½ teaspoon sugar and ¼ teaspoon monosodium glutamate. Mix well.

Now add the ham and the slightly scrambled eggs, mixing and breaking eggs into little pieces in the rice. Serve hot.

TIPS

It is important that the rice be thoroughly cold before cooking begins—otherwise the grains of rice will stick together and the result will be a gooey mess.

Cooked chicken may be substituted for ham to make Chicken Fried Rice, and roast beef may be used for Beef Fried Rice.

- ## WONTON SOUP
  4 SERVINGS

INGREDIENTS

> 3 cups chicken broth
> 16 wontons
> 1 scallion, chopped
> 1 tablespoon soy sauce
> ½ teaspoon salt
> white pepper to taste

PREPARATION OF WONTONS

1. *Making the wrapping (known as "skin"):*

> 1 cup flour
> 1 egg
> ½ teaspoon salt

Sift flour and salt into a mixing bowl. Break the egg into the flour and knead. Sprinkle a little flour on a breadboard and turn dough on board. Knead until smooth. Cover dough with wet towel and let stand for 20 minutes. Roll dough out paper thin. Cut into 4″ squares.

2. *Making the filling:*

> ½ pound ground pork
> 1 tablespoon dry sherry
> 1. tablespoon soy sauce
> ½ teaspoon salt
> ½ teaspoon sugar
> ¼ teaspoon monosodium glutamate

Mix all ingredients in a bowl and use as filling.

3. *How to wrap wontons:*

Put ½ teaspoon of filling just off-center on each 4″ square (Fig. 1). Fold over at the center. Gently press the edges together (Fig. 2). Fold in half again lengthwise

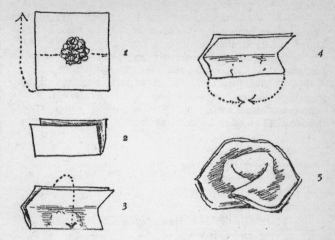

(Fig. 3). Pull the two corners one over the other and press them together with a little water (Fig. 4). A properly wrapped wonton resembles a nurse's cap (Fig. 5).

COOKING PROCEDURES

Boil 3 quarts of water. Add the 16 wontons and bring to a boil again. Wontons will float to the surface.

Add ½ cup cold water and bring to a boil once more. This last boil insures that the filling will be thoroughly cooked. When wontons float to the surface of the water again, they are ready. Drain and reserve.

Heat the chicken broth, adding 1 tablespoon soy sauce and 1 teaspoon salt.

Gently drop the cooked wontons into the broth. Add scallion and serve.

TIPS

In the larger American cities where there are Chinese food stores, wonton wrappings are available in pound packages. Using these will save a great deal of time. The unused wrapping can be kept in the refrigerator wrapped in foil for at least a week. They can be kept frozen for even longer.

Shrimp Wontons are made with a filling containing chopped uncooked shrimps instead of pork. These are very delicious.

Wontons may be served in other ways than in broth. After wontons have been cooked in boiling water, drain and cool; then pan fry immediately, or, if desired, the following day. To eat, dip in sauce made of equal portions of soy sauce and red-wine vinegar.

Wontons can be made in large batches, arranged in cake or candy boxes and kept frozen for several weeks. When you use them, cook them in boiling water without thawing. They taste as good as freshly made wontons.

• EGG DROP SOUP
4 SERVINGS

INGREDIENTS

3 cups clear chicken broth
1 cup water
1 teaspoon salt
1 scallion
1 egg
1 tablespoon cornstarch
white pepper to taste

PREPARATION

Wash and cut the scallion into ⅛" pieces.
Beat the egg thoroughly.
Dissolve 1 tablespoon cornstarch in 2 tablespoons cold water.

COOKING PROCEDURES

Heat 3 cups chicken broth and 1 cup water in a saucepan until it boils.
Add salt and stir a few times.
Add cornstarch slowly until it gradually becomes thickened.
Add the scallion and mix a few times.
Gently stir in the beaten egg. Turn off heat immediately.
Serve. Let each person add pepper to his taste.

TIPS

This soup can be made with chicken broth or beef broth. It is important to turn off heat completely *immediately* after the egg is stirred in, so that the egg will float like a cloud to the surface.

● GROUND STEAK WITH PEAS
    4 SERVINGS

INGREDIENTS

12 *ounces very lean ground steak*
1 *package frozen peas*
2 *tablespoons peanut or corn oil*
2 *tablespoons soy sauce*
1 *tablespoon dry sherry*
1 *teaspoon sugar*
2 *teaspoons cornstarch*

PREPARATION

Thaw the peas.
Dissolve the 2 teaspoons cornstarch in 1 tablespoon water.

COOKING PROCEDURES

Heat the 2 tablespoons oil in a frying pan over high flame.
Add the ground steak, stirring for about 2 minutes, or until red color disappears.
Add 2 tablespoons soy sauce, 1 tablespoon dry sherry and 1 teaspoon sugar. Mix thoroughly.
Add the peas, mix well and cook for 3 minutes.
Thicken with cornstarch dissolved in water. Serve hot.

TIPS

This is an easy recipe which takes a very short time to prepare. It is cooked entirely over a high flame. Fresh peas are preferred during the season. It is best to parboil fresh peas before using.

• MOO GOO GAI PIEN
4 SERVINGS

INGREDIENTS

2 *double chicken breasts*
1 *4-ounce can white button mushrooms*
1 *sweet green pepper*
2 *tablespoons peanut or corn oil*
1 *teaspoon salt*
¼ *teaspoon white pepper*
1 *teaspoon cornstarch*

PREPARATION

Skin and bone chicken breasts and cut into slices 1" x 1" x ¼".

Mix with the chicken ½ teaspoon salt, ¼ teaspoon pepper and 1 teaspoon cornstarch.

Cut sweet pepper into pieces approximately the same size as chicken.

COOKING PROCEDURES

Heat oil in frying pan over high flame.

Add the seasoned chicken and stir continuously for about 2 minutes. The chicken will turn white.

Add sweet pepper and mushrooms. Mix thoroughly. If the mixture is too dry, add 1 tablespoon of the mushroom juice from can. Serve hot.

TIPS

Start with fresh, uncooked chicken breasts for a really tender and tasty dish. However, cooked leftover chicken breast can be used with good results. In that case, do not sprinkle with cornstarch, but dissolve the cornstarch and use it rather as thickening, at the very last.

• BARBECUED SPARERIBS
4 SERVINGS

INGREDIENTS

2 *pounds baby pork ribs*
2 *scallions cut in 2" pieces*

2 *cloves garlic, slightly crushed*
1 *tablespoon chili sauce*
1 *tablespoon tomato ketchup*
2 *tablespoons soy sauce*
2 *tablespoons dry sherry*
1 *tablespoon corn syrup*
½ *teaspoon salt*
1 *tablespoon honey*

PREPARATION

Marinate the baby ribs in a flat pan with 2 scallions, 2 cloves of garlic, 1 tablespoon chili sauce, 2 tablespoons soy sauce, 1 tablespoon tomato ketchup, 2 tablespoons sherry, 1 tablespoon syrup, and ½ teaspoon salt for about 2 hours. After an hour, baste and turn over.

Brush the ribs on both sides with honey.

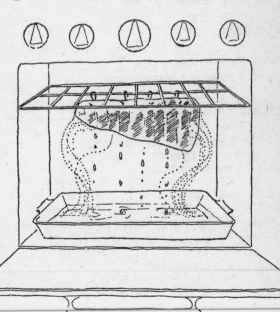

COOKING PROCEDURES

Hook the ribs to the cross bars of the shelves in your oven (see illustration page 57) and roast for 30 minutes at 275 degrees, for another 30 minutes at 300 degrees and finally for 10 minutes at 400 degrees. Serve hot or cold and cut for appetizer or hors d'oeuvre.

TIPS

Spareribs may be made the day before and heated before serving, unless they are to be served cold.

Make hooks from wire coat hangers by cutting wire into pieces 3″ long and bending at both ends. Hook one end onto the cross bar and the other end onto the ribs. Each rack of ribs should have 2 hooks attached to the thick ends. Set a large pan with water in the oven to catch the drippings and also to give out moisture to keep the ribs from becoming too dry.

- *SHRIMP EGG ROLLS*
  MAKES 18 ROLLS

INGREDIENTS

FOR EGG-ROLL WRAPPERS:

2 cups flour
½ teaspoon salt
¾ cup water

FOR FILLING:

½ pound uncooked shrimps
½ pound fresh bean sprouts (or 1 can)
4 cups finely chopped celery
⅓ cup sliced button mushrooms
2 teaspoons salt
½ teaspoon sugar
½ teaspoon monosodium glutamate
1 teaspoon sherry
½ teaspoon cornstarch
3 tablespoons peanut or corn oil
oil for deep frying

PREPARATION

OF EGG-ROLL WRAPPERS:

Add ½ teaspoon salt to 2 cups flour and sift twice. Mix with ¾ cup water. Knead until smooth. Sprinkle flour generously on a breadboard and roll out dough paper thin (about 27″ square). Cut into eighteen 9″ triangles.

OF FILLING:

Shell, devein, rinse and drain the shrimps. Cut into ½″ pieces.

Mix in a bowl with 1 teaspoon sherry, ½ teaspoon salt, ¼ teaspoon monosodium glutamate and ½ teaspoon cornstarch.

If canned bean sprouts are used, drain sprouts and rinse in cold water 2 or 3 times. If fresh bean sprouts are used, just wash and drain.

Cut the mushroom slices into smaller pieces.

Heat 1 tablespoon oil in a frying pan over high flame and add shrimps Stir and cook over high flame until all shrimps turn pink. Place in dish and set aside.

In a clean frying pan heat 2 tablespoons oil and add celery. Stir rapidly over high flame for about 2 minutes.

Add 1½ teaspoons salt, ½ teaspoon sugar and ¼ teaspoon monosodium glutamate and mix well. Cook for 5 minutes over medium flame.

Add mushrooms and mix thoroughly. Then add mushroom juice.

Now add bean sprouts and mix a few times.

Last, add the cooked shrimps and after stirring a few times turn into a colander and let all juice drain off. Cool thoroughly before using as filling.

HOW TO WRAP EGG ROLLS:

Place a triangle of dough on a board with corner A at the top of the board (Fig. 1).

Place ¼ cup of cooled filling in the center and fold corners B and C toward the center until they overlap (Fig. 2).

Roll up and continue to roll until it reaches corner A. With a little cold water seal corner A securely to the roll (Fig. 3).

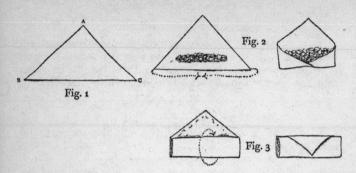

Fig. 1

Fig. 2

Fig. 3

COOKING PROCEDURES

Heat oil to 375 degrees and deep fry the egg rolls one at a time for 3 to 5 minutes, until each is golden brown. Cut each roll into 3 or 4 pieces. Serve hot.

TIPS

If the 2 cups of flour do not yield 18 rolls, or you need a larger quantity than 18, duplicate the recipe and make 18 more. May I suggest, as I did for wontons, that you buy wrappers whenever you can. This will save you a great deal of time.

Egg rolls can be made well in advance of serving. Deep fry for 1 minute and allow to drain on paper towels. When serving time arrives, deep fry again until golden brown.

2. MENUS USING INGREDIENTS FROM AMERICAN MARKETS

WHAT MAKES A CHINESE DISH CHINESE?

MENU I

Boiled Rice, the Chinese Way
Soy Sauce Spiced Beef
Spinach, Chinese Style
Jasmine Tea
Fresh Fruits

MENU II

Sweet-Sour Pineapple Pork
Fried Rice with Ham and
    Eggs
String Beans, Chinese Style
Black Tea
Fortune Cookies

MENU III

Fried Noodles with Pork
    Shreds
Chicken Breast with Sweet
    Pepper
Salad à la Chu
Green Tea
Almond Cookies

MENU IV

Soy Sauce Rice
Shrimps with Cucumber
Broccoli, Chinese Style
Oolong Tea
Preserved Kumquats

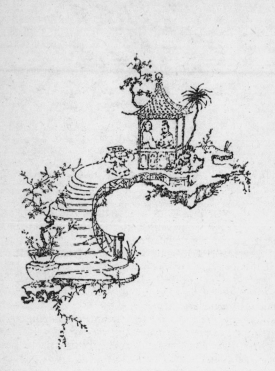

What Makes
a Chinese Dish Chinese?

ON ENCOUNTERING an interesting-looking Oriental dish, how can you determine whether or not it is Chinese? The lazy way is simply to take someone's word for it. But if this trusting approach turns out to be unsatisfactory, here are some additional clues that will help you form your own conclusions.

You can begin by identifying the ingredients. Does the dish contain ingredients that are considered typically Chinese? If so, the object of your investigation is probably a Chinese dish. For example, such ingredients as bamboo shoots, bean curd, winter melon, or shark's fins should give you some clue as to the nationality of that particular dish.

But a dish with ingredients that are not typically Chinese may still be a Chinese dish—if it is prepared in the Chinese way. Chinese cookery is distinctive and markedly different from the cookery of, say, France, Italy or the United States. As mentioned earlier, chop suey earns its right to be called a Chinese dish under this more liberal definition.

Students of Chinese cookery should become completely familiar with the basic methods of preparing and cooking Chinese foods.

The recipes in the four menus that follow are designed to help you put into practice the techniques of preparation,

cutting and cooking discussed in Part I. They are carefully planned so that they call for only those ingredients
obtainable in practically every American market or grocery
store. In addition, they are planned with balanced food
values in mind.

The organization is in menu form because it is a Chinese
custom to serve at least three or four dishes at a family-
style meal (for a family of four to six). Such a meal nor-
mally includes (1) a meat dish (of pork, more often than
not, since pork is the favorite meat of the Chinese); (2)
a seafood dish (perhaps fish or shrimps); and (3) any vegetable in season. If a fourth item is added, it will perhaps
be an egg dish, to round out the menu. The aim is to plan
a complete meal that is simple, yet varied.

The menus are arranged, in general, in order of time
required for preparation and cooking. The time given includes *both* preparation and cooking. It goes without saying
—but let's say it anyway just to be absolutely sure—that
those dishes which require the longest preparation and cooking time should be started first. The trick is to have *all*
the dishes ready for the table at the same time.

A word of advice for the beginning student of Chinese
cookery. Before starting on the menus, read Part I again
and be sure you are thoroughly familiar with the various
methods of cutting and cooking. Next read through all
recipes included in the menu you are planning to serve.
You'll discover that in Chinese cookery much more time is
spent on the preparation than on the actual cooking. Once
you are ready to heat up the pan, the rest is surprisingly
easy. Give these menus a try and surprise yourself and your
family with your culinary creations.

MENU I
FOR 4 PERSONS

Boiled Rice, the Chinese Way
Soy Sauce Spiced Beef
Spinach, Chinese Style
Jasmine Tea (See The Story of Tea, *pages* 30–33)
Fresh Fruits

● *BOILED RICE, THE CHINESE WAY*
  TIME: 50 MINUTES

INGREDIENTS

   1 *cup long-grain rice*
   1¾ *cups cold water*

PREPARATION

   Place rice in strainer and rinse thoroughly in cold running water. Drain.

COOKING PROCEDURES

   Place rice in a 2-quart saucepan and add 1¾ cups cold water. Bring to boil over high flame (about 5 minutes).

   Turn flame to low, cover and let simmer for 20 minutes, until dry. Turn off flame.

   Allow the rice to stand, covered, for another 20 minutes.

   Stir well while rice is still hot so that it will be flaky and each grain will be separate. Makes 3 cups of cooked rice.

TIPS

   Rice must be rinsed before cooking to get rid of any excess starch so that it does not burn while cooking. Do not stir the rice during cooking or it will stick to the bottom of the pan. The Chinese do not add salt or butter when cooking rice.

   If rice other than long-grain is used, decrease the amount of water to 1½ cups. Long-grain rice, which most Chinese prefer, absorbs more water and yields a larger quantity of cooked rice from the same amount of raw rice than the shorter-grained varieties.

   Cooked rice can be kept warm in the oven. Cold cooked rice can be used to make fried rice. This will keep for a few days in the refrigerator and can be reheated with good results.

● SOY SAUCE SPICED BEEF
TIME: 45 MINUTES

INGREDIENTS

1 *pound boneless stewing beef*
2 *tablespoons peanut or corn oil*
2 *tablespoons dry sherry*
3 *tablespoons soy sauce*
1 *teaspoon sugar*
2 *scallions*
½ *teaspoon star anise or 5 drops anise extract*
(*may be purchased at drugstore if unavailable at market*)

PREPARATION

Wash beef and cut into 1″ cubes.
Wash scallions and cut into 2″ pieces, using both green and white parts.

COOKING PROCEDURES

Heat 2 tablespoons peanut or corn oil in a saucepan over a high flame. Add the beef cubes. Keep turning them until all sides are well seared.

Add 2 tablespoons dry sherry, 3 tablespoons soy sauce and 1 teaspoon sugar. Mix well and cook for 2 to 3 minutes.

Stir in the scallions and add 1 cup cold water. Bring to boil.

Reduce flame to medium, cover pan and cook for 20 minutes. Stir a few times during this process.

Stir in star anise or anise extract. Reduce flame to low, cover and continue cooking for another 20 minutes. Serve hot or cold.

TIPS

This dish can be prepared one or two days ahead and warmed in the oven or over the burner before serving. It can be frozen and reheated without thawing.

- ### SPINACH, CHINESE STYLE
  TIME: 5 MINUTES

INGREDIENTS

> 1 *pound fresh spinach, or 10-ounce package pre-washed spinach*
> 1 *clove garlic*
> 1 *teaspoon salt*
> ½ *teaspoon sugar*
> ¼ *teaspoon monosodium glutamate (optional)*
> 2 *tablespoons peanut or corn oil*

PREPARATION

Wash and drain the spinach, removing any wilted leaves.

Crush the clove of garlic.

COOKING PROCEDURES

Heat the 2 tablespoons of oil with the crushed garlic in a saucepan over high flame.

Add spinach and stir until the oil is thoroughly mixed with the spinach. Discard garlic.

Add 1 teaspoon salt, ½ teaspoon sugar and ¼ teaspoon monosodium glutamate. Stir again. Cook for 2 minutes. Serve hot.

TIPS

Since spinach cooks only a short time, try to cook it at the very end of your preparation of the meal so that it will retain its tenderness and green color. All leafy vegetables such as water cress, romaine lettuce, Boston lettuce, celery cabbage and Chinese greens (*bok choy*) can be cooked the same way.

- ### JASMINE TEA

This is the most popular of the scented teas and can be bought in many specialty stores. When purchased in a cardboard box, it should immediately be transferred to a canister or a jar to preserve its freshness and flavor.

●   *FRESH FRUITS*

If desired, any fresh fruit or combination of fruits, served in the American manner, may be offered at the end of a Chinese meal. The Chinese are not great eaters of sweet pastries either as dessert or as between-meal snacks.

MENU II
FOR 4 PERSONS

Sweet-Sour Pineapple Pork
Fried Rice with Ham and Eggs
String Beans, Chinese Style
Black Tea (See The Story of Tea, *pages* 30–33)
Fortune Cookies

• SWEET-SOUR PINEAPPLE PORK
TIME: 45 MINUTES

INGREDIENTS

> 1 pound (any cut) boneless pork, or 6 lean pork chops
> 8 ounces canned pineapple chunks with juice
> 4 ounces sweet mixed pickles in chunks with juice
> 1 medium-sized tomato
> 2 cloves garlic
> 2 tablespoons soy sauce
> 1 teaspoon dry sherry
> ½ teaspoon salt
> 3 teaspoons cornstarch
> 2 cups vegetable oil for deep frying
> 1 tablespoon oil for sauce

PREPARATION

Cut pork into 1″ cubes and mix them in a bowl with 1 teaspoon dry sherry, ½ teaspoon salt and 1 teaspoon cornstarch. (The other 2 teaspoons of cornstarch are for thickening the sauce.) Let stand for 20 minutes.

Drain the pineapple and the sweet mixed pickles, saving juice of both.

Wash and cut the tomato into 8 wedges.

Crush the 2 cloves of garlic with the side of a Chinese cleaver.

Dissolve the remaining 2 teaspoons of cornstarch in 1 tablespoon of cold water.

COOKING PROCEDURES

Deep fry the pork in oil at about 375 degrees for 6 minutes, or until golden brown. Drain the oil off and put pork on a platter. Keep warm.

Make sauce and pour over pork.

COOKING PROCEDURES FOR SAUCE

Heat 1 tablespoon oil with crushed garlic in a saucepan over a high flame for 1 minute. Remove garlic.

Add juice of pineapple and pickles, then add 2 tablespoons soy sauce. Bring mixture to boil. Add pickles and pineapple chunks.

When the mixture comes to a boil again, thicken with the dissolved cornstarch.

Mix in the tomato wedges and the sauce is ready for use.

TIPS

In deep frying the pork, it is best to use a strainer 3″ in diameter, so that the pork can be lifted out of the oil briefly after 3 minutes, and then put back in the oil again to finish cooking. Because it has cooled slightly in the interval, the pork will be well cooked, but still tender and juicy. Always remember to cook pork *thoroughly*. The bones from the pork chops can be used to make stock.

Vinegar and sugar are often used in the making of sweet-sour sauce. But a sauce made with juices of pineapple and sweet mixed pickles has a more delicate, richer flavor.

This same sauce may be used to make Sweet-Sour Pineapple Shrimps or Sweet-Sour Pineapple Fish. If shrimps are used, boil, then shell and devein them. Drop the shrimps into the sauce and cook for 1 minute until they are warm. If fish fillets are used, proceed as with pork. Decrease the time for deep frying to about 3 minutes.

● *FRIED RICE WITH HAM AND EGGS*
TIME: 15 MINUTES

INGREDIENTS

3 *cups cold boiled rice*
2 *eggs*
2 *scallions*
¼ *cup diced boiled ham*
¼ *cup diced cooked carrots*
¼ *cup cooked peas*
1 *teaspoon salt*
4 *tablespoons peanut or corn oil*

PREPARATION

Beat the eggs and lightly scramble with 1 tablespoon oil. (Do not add milk or water to eggs.) Set aside.

Wash and cut the scallions (white and green parts) into ¼" pieces.

COOKING PROCEDURES

Heat 3 tablespoons oil over a high flame in a heavy frying pan and add scallions. Mix a few times.

Add rice and salt and mix thoroughly.

Add ham, carrots and peas and stir well.

Add eggs. Mix well and serve.

TIPS

The rice must be cold before you fry it in order to get the best results. Cook the rice at least several hours before you plan to use it. Break up rice while still hot and let it stand until you are ready to put it in the frying pan.

This is a basic fried-rice recipe. For variation, cold diced beef, veal, turkey or chicken may be substituted for ham.

Leftover fried rice may be stored in the refrigerator and reheated in the oven without additional water or oil. It can also be frozen.

● *STRING BEANS, CHINESE STYLE*
  TIME: 15 MINUTES

INGREDIENTS

1 pound fresh string beans
1 teaspoon salt
¼ teaspoon monosodium glutamate (optional)
2 tablespoons peanut or corn oil

PREPARATION

Break beans into 2" pieces. Wash and drain.

COOKING PROCEDURES

Heat 2 tablespoons oil in a saucepan over a high flame. Add string beans and stir until beans are coated with oil.

Add 1 teaspoon salt and ¼ teaspoon monosodium glutamate and stir some more.

Add ¼ cup cold water, cover pan, reduce flame to medium and cook for 10 minutes. Stir again.

Cook with cover on until all liquid is absorbed. Serve hot.

TIPS

This is a typical method for cooking nonleafy vegetables such as beans, carrots, cauliflower, broccoli, Brussels sprouts. Vegetables in this group can be cooked beforehand and reheated in the same pan before using. If vegetables are to be reheated, do not cover the pan after the cooking is finished; keeping the pan uncovered will help preserve their natural color.

- *BLACK TEA*

Black tea goes well with this menu. This is a fermented tea produced in China as well as India and other Asian countries. Because the color of this tea is actually red, the Chinese commonly call it "red tea"; why others call it black is a mystery.

- *FORTUNE COOKIES*

Fortune cookies are unknown in China, but they have become as popular in America as chop suey. You can buy them in Chinese food stores and in many supermarkets. But if you want to make your own fortune cookies you can have the fun of making up your own fortunes, too. Here is a recipe.

INGREDIENTS

    1 *cup flour*
    1 *egg, slightly beaten*
    ¼ *cup sugar*
    1 *teaspoon vanilla extract*
    1 *cup water*

PREPARATION AND BAKING

Mix all ingredients in a bowl and let stand for 10 minutes.

Heat a Krumkaker Iron (available from Scandinavian specialty stores) to 375 degrees. Pour 1 tablespoon of the mixture into the iron. Heat from 3 to 4 minutes; turn the iron and heat the other side for another 3 minutes.

Remove cooky from iron and, while still warm, fold cooky in half and then bend over again to form a fortune cooky. (Make up your own fortunes to fit the occasion, write them on small slips of paper and enclose 1 slip in each cooky before folding.)

MENU III
FOR 4 PERSONS

Fried Noodles with Pork Shreds
Chicken Breast with Sweet Pepper
Salad à la Chu
Green Tea (See The Story of Tea, *pages 30–33)*
Almond Cookies

• FRIED NOODLES WITH PORK SHREDS
TIME: 50 MINUTES

INGREDIENTS

> ½ pound thin spaghetti No. 9
> ½ pound (any cut) boneless pork
> 1 pound celery cabbage
>   (also called Chinese cabbage)
> 2 ounces fresh mushrooms, or
>   1 small can sliced mushrooms
> 2 eggs
> 1½ teaspoons salt
> 1 teaspoon sugar
> 3 tablepoons soy sauce
> 6 tablespoons peanut or corn oil

PREPARATION

Cut the pork into shreds (2" x ¼" x ¼").

Cut the celery cabbage into similar shreds.

Wash and slice fresh mushrooms. If canned mushrooms are used, drain the mushrooms and save the juice.

Beat the two eggs. Heat 1 tablespoon oil in a heavy frying pan over a high flame and make a big "pancake" with the two eggs; do not stir but let the egg set. When cool, cut into Julienne strips.

Bring to a boil 2 quarts of water and add 1 teaspoon salt. Drop in the spaghetti. Cook for 8 minutes. Drain and immediately run under cold water until thoroughly cold. Drain again. Mix 2 tablespoons oil with the cold spaghetti and set aside until ready for frying.

COOKING PROCEDURES FOR PORK MIXTURE

Heat 1 tablespoon oil in a frying pan over a high flame. Add pork and stir for a minute, until all pork shreds turn white. Add 3 tablespoons soy sauce and 1 teaspoon sugar and stir a few times. Add mushroom slices and celery cabbage and mix well. Add 2 tablespoons water or canned mushroom juice, cover, turn flame to medium and cook for 8-10 minutes.

COOKING PROCEDURES FOR FRIED NOODLES

In another frying pan, over a high flame, heat 2 tablespoons oil and add spaghetti. Spread the spaghetti evenly and let it cook for about 2 minutes, then turn. Mix and cook for another 2 to 3 minutes. (Only part of the spaghetti will be fried.) Sprinkle ½ teaspoon salt over the spaghetti. Mix lightly. Pour in about 4/5 of the pork mixture and mix well. Put on a platter. Top with rest of pork mixture and over this place the egg strips. Serve hot.

TIPS

To cut pork into thin slices or to shred, freeze the pork slightly so that it will be firm and easy to handle. The shreds should be cut as fine as possible.

Thin spaghetti No. 9 is the nearest thing to the noodles that we use in China when making fried noodles.

Noodles can be prepared and cooked beforehand. Just warm the noodles before serving and add the pork mixture, also warmed, and the egg strips. Whatever is left over can be reheated in the oven the following day. This dish can also be cooked and frozen. To serve, thaw and heat.

Celery cabbage is most often used in salads. The combination in this recipe is the basic method of preparing noodles. It is the real "chow mein" of China. This recipe can be adapted for Fried Noodles with Shrimps, Fried Noodles with Roast Beef and Fried Noodles with Chicken.

● *CHICKEN BREAST WITH SWEET PEPPER*
TIME: 15 MINUTES

INGREDIENTS

2 *large double chicken breasts*
1 *medium-sized sweet pepper*
2 *tablespoons peanut or corn oil*
2 *tablespoons dry sherry*
2 *teaspoons salt*
¼ *teaspoon monosodium glutamate*
1 *tablespoon cornstarch*

PREPARATION

Cut the skinned and boned chicken into 1" cubes. Mix chicken with 1 teaspoon salt, 2 tablespoons sherry, ¼ teaspoon monosodium glutamate and 1 tablespoon cornstarch.

Wash the pepper, remove the seeds and cut into 1" squares.

COOKING PROCEDURES

Heat 2 tablespoons oil in a frying pan over a high flame. Add chicken and stir briskly for about 2 minutes. The chicken will turn white and each piece will be separate.

Mix in the pepper squares and stir a few times.

Add 1 teaspoon salt and stir again for about 1 minute. If too dry, add 1 tablespoon water. Stir a few more times. Serve hot.

TIPS

Note that soy sauce is not used in this dish; its goodness is in the flavor of the chicken and green pepper. Many Chinese dishes are made without soy sauce and depend entirely on the natural flavor of the meats and vegetables used.

- SALAD À LA CHU
  TIME: 45 MINUTES

INGREDIENTS

1 bunch celery
1 bunch radishes
2 tablespoons soy sauce
2 teaspoons peanut or corn oil
1 teaspoon salt
½ teaspoon sugar
¼ teaspoon monosodium glutamate

PREPARATION

Wash and clean the radishes. Crush them slightly with the side of the cleaver so that they will remain whole. Add salt and let stand for 30 minutes.

Wash celery and cut into ½″ pieces, discarding the leaves. Soak in ice water until ready for use.

Mix the 2 tablespoons soy sauce, 2 teaspoons oil, ½ teaspoon sugar and ¼ teaspoon monosodium glutamate in a bowl.

When ready to serve, drain radishes and celery and mix with the soy sauce-oil dressing.

TIPS

Radishes and celery can be prepared and left in the refrigerator. The dressing can also be mixed ahead and stored in a jar. The actual combining should be done just before serving to insure color and crunchiness.

● *GREEN TEA*

This is an unfermented tea with a very delicate flavor and very light color. Use the same amount of tea for each cup as with any other tea. Steep for a few minutes before serving.

● *ALMOND COOKIES*
   TIME: 35 MINUTES

INGREDIENTS

   3 *cups sifted flour*
   1 *cup sugar*
   1 *cup shortening*
   4 *tablespoons corn syrup, molasses or honey*
   1 *egg*
   3 *tablespoons almond extract*
   1½ *teaspoons baking soda*
   1 *cup blanched almonds*

Preparation

Cream shortening and sugar together. Then add the beaten egg.

Slowly add flour, baking soda, almond extract and syrup to the mixture and mix until smooth.

Take a small piece of the dough and roll it into a ball. Continue until all dough has been used.

Flatten each ball into a thick cooky. Place an almond in the center of each.

Baking Procedure

Bake on a greased cooky sheet in the oven at 375 degrees for about 20 minutes. Makes about 4 dozen cookies.

Tips

Almond cookies can be made several days ahead, or they can be wrapped in foil and frozen. They will keep in the freezer for several months.

Large almonds may be split, ½ almond to a cooky.

In China, lard is used in making almond cookies, but margarine may be substituted if preferred.

MENU IV
FOR 4 PERSONS

Soy Sauce Rice
Shrimp with Cucumber
Broccoli, Chinese Style
Oolong Tea (See The Story of Tea, *pages 30–33)*
Preserved Kumquats

- ### *SOY SAUCE RICE*
  TIME: 55 MINUTES

INGREDIENTS

- 1 *cup long-grain rice*
- 2 *tablespoons peanut or corn oil*
- 3 *tablespoons soy sauce*
- 2 *tablespoons chopped scallions*
- 2 *tablespoons diced pimento*
- ½ *teaspoon sugar*
- ¼ *teaspoon monosodium glutamate*

PREPARATION

Place rice in strainer and rinse thoroughly under cold running water. Drain dry.

COOKING PROCEDURES

Place rice in a 2-quart pan and add 1¾ cups cold water. Bring to boil over a high flame.

Turn flame to low and let simmer for 20 minutes. Turn off flame.

Allow the rice to stand for another 20 minutes.

With a fork or a pair of chopsticks stir the cooked rice. Stir in the 2 tablespoons oil, 3 tablespoons soy sauce, ½ teaspoon sugar, ¼ teaspoon monosodium glutamate, 2 tablespoons diced pimento and 2 tablespoons chopped scallions. Mix well.

TIPS

Do not stir the rice while cooking or it will stick to the bottom of the pan. Stir well only when it is done and before the other ingredients are added, to separate grains. Rice can be prepared in advance and reheated before using. Soy Sauce Rice can be frozen and kept for several weeks. When using rice that has been frozen, warm it in the oven.

- ### SHRIMP WITH CUCUMBER
  TIME: 30 MINUTES

INGREDIENTS

> 1 *pound uncooked shrimps*
> 2 *medium-sized cucumbers*
> 3 *tablespoons peanut or corn oil*
> 1 *tablespoon dry sherry*
> 2 *teaspoons salt*
> 1 *teaspoon sugar*
> 2 *teaspoons cornstarch*

PREPARATION

Shell and devein the shrimps. Wash and drain. Cut each shrimp in half lengthwise, then cut each half into 2 or 3 pieces crosswise.

Combine shrimps with 1 tablespoon sherry, 1 teaspoon salt, 1 teaspoon sugar and 2 teaspoons cornstarch.

Peel the cucumbers. Quarter lengthwise and scoop out seeds. Then cut into 1″ pieces.

COOKING PROCEDURES

Over a high flame in a saucepan, sauté the cucumber with 1 tablespoon oil. Add 1 teaspoon salt and stir until the cucumber is slightly transparent (3 to 5 minutes).

In another saucepan, over a high flame, sauté the shrimps with 2 tablespoons oil. Stir continuously until the shrimps turn pink.

Add cucumber, mix and cook for 2 to 3 minutes more. Serve hot.

TIPS

The cucumbers can be cooked beforehand, but the shrimps should not be cooked in advance, as this will tend to overcook them when they are reheated.

• BROCCOLI, CHINESE STYLE
TIME: 20 MINUTES

INGREDIENTS

> 1 *small bunch broccoli*
> 2 *tablespoons peanut or corn oil*
> 1 *teaspoon salt*
> ½ *teaspoon sugar*
> ¼ *teaspoon monosodium glutamate*

PREPARATION

Wash broccoli and cut the flowerets off the stems.
Peel off stringy outsides of stems and then cut stems into 1″ pieces.

Parboil stems and flowerets. Rinse in cold water and drain.

COOKING PROCEDURES

In a saucepan over a high flame heat 2 tablespoons oil. Add broccoli and stir until well covered with oil.

Add 1 teaspoon salt, ½ teaspoon sugar and ¼ teaspoon monosodium glutamate. Mix well.

Add ½ cup water, cover pan, turn flame down to medium and cook for 5 minutes. Stir.

Cook over a high flame, uncovered, until the liquid is almost all absorbed. Serve warm.

TIPS

When cooking broccoli and other green vegetables, never lift the cover more than once; otherwise the green color of the vegetable will turn yellowish. If the vegetable must be reheated, cook *without cover*. In Chinese cooking, eye appeal is an important requirement.

• PRESERVED KUMQUATS
Time: 45 Minutes

Ingredients

> 1 *quart fresh kumquats*
> 2 *cups sugar*
> 1 *cup water*

Preparation

Wash kumquats. Pierce each kumquat so that it will not burst in cooking.

Cooking Procedures

Bring sugar and water to boil in a saucepan and let simmer for 10 minutes.

Add kumquats to syrup and cook gently for 30 minutes, or until tender.

Place in sterilized screw-top glass jar and cover.

Tips

Preserved kumquats are available in specialty shops, but when fresh kumquats are available, they will be much more delicious if you preserve them yourself.

3. MENUS USING INGREDIENTS FROM CHINESE FOOD STORES

FAMILY COOKING, CHINESE STYLE

MENU I

Fish Ball-Water Cress Soup
Flank Steak in Oyster Sauce
Chicken-Mung Bean Sprout
  Salad
Pork Shreds with Dried Bean
  Curd and Mushrooms
Boiled Rice
Tea
Almond Float

MENU II

Chicken Velvet Corn Soup
Millionaire Chicken
Tan Chiao (Half-Moon
  Omelet) with Peas
Red Cabbage Salad
Boiled Rice
Tea
Lichee Delight

MENU III

Cellophane Noodle and Meat
  Ball Soup
Shrimps in Lobster Sauce
Agar-Agar Ham Salad
Chicken with Nuts in Hoisin
  Sauce
Boiled Rice
Tea
Golden Surprise (Sweet Filled
  Wontons)

MENU IV

Cucumber-Pork Slice Soup
Roast Pork
Asparagus Salad
Steamed Sea Bass
Boiled Rice
Tea
Individual Eight Precious
  Pudding

MENU V

Chinese Mustard Green and
  Bean Curd Soup
Five Diced Fish
Mo-Shu-Ro, Pork Dish
Cucumber Salad
Boiled Rice
Tea
Assorted Chinese Fruits

MENU VI

Winter Melon and Ham Soup
Szechuen Pork
Ground Steak with Onions
Anchovy Lettuce Salad
Boiled Rice
Tea
Almond "Tea"

MENU VII

Sour and Hot Soup
Lobster with Black Bean
  Sauce
String Beans in Special Bean
  Curd Sauce
Cellophane Noodles with
  Pork Shreds
Boiled Rice
Tea
Date and Sesame Seed Ping

MENU VIII

Abalone and Chicken Soup
Sweet-Sour Fish
Cucumber Stuffed with
  Ground Pork
Chinese Greens with Bamboo
  Shoots and Mushrooms
Boiled Rice
Tea
Chinese Steamed Cake

Family Cooking, Chinese Style

Now THAT you have learned the basic techniques of Chinese cooking and have tried some of the simpler menus in the previous sections, the next step is the preparation of a complete Chinese family-style meal. This section is organized into eight complete menus for just this purpose. The menus usually include a soup, a heavy meat dish, a light meat dish, a vegetable or salad dish, rice, tea and dessert.

A few explanations may be in order for some of the terms used. In Chinese cooking, as you already know, many dishes call for a combination of meat and vegetables. Thus, a "heavy" meat dish merely means that a greater proportion of meat is used in relation to the vegetables, while a "light" meat dish uses comparatively less meat to vegetables.

On the matter of salads, we Chinese do not actually have salad dishes as Americans know them. For health reasons, the eating of uncooked vegetables can be a hazardous business in China. The Chinese do, however, have certain cooked vegetable dishes that are served much as Americans would serve salads. Some of these are included in the following menus to add still another touch of variety to your Chinese meal.

Desserts are practically unknown in China. The Chinese, generally speaking, are not overly fond of sweets. The closest thing to dessert in China is the serving of fresh fruits at the end of the meal. But for those Americans who might feel that a meal is not a meal without dessert, I have included a few Chinese sweet dishes. (Actually, these are sweets that are served between courses at a Chinese banquet, but they can be pressed into service as dessert dishes at an ordinary meal.)

One other matter bears mentioning. To the Chinese, soup is not the first course of the meal. We serve soup as a dish which is to be sipped throughout the entire course of the meal, almost as if it were a beverage. The only other beverage commonly served is tea—hot tea. Cold beverages are almost never served in China.

The menus in this section have been carefully selected for variety and nutritional values. In contrast to the recipes in the previous section, some of the ingredients required here may not be available at an ordinary American food store. The ingredients, however, can be obtained from Chinese stores in many of the large cities in the United States. Some of these stores are listed on pages 39–40.

Wherever necessary, I have included under *Tips* suggestions with each recipe which I hope will help you to use and store Chinese food items. Ingredients that may be changed or substituted are also mentioned here.

MENU I
For 4 Persons

Fish Ball–Water Cress Soup
Flank Steak in Oyster Sauce
Chicken–Mung Bean Sprout Salad
Pork Shreds with Dried Bean Curd and
   Mushrooms
Boiled Rice (see page 66)
Tea
Almond Float

• FISH BALL–WATER CRESS SOUP
TIME: 10 MINUTES

INGREDIENTS

> 1 *small can Scandinavian fish balls*
> 1 *bunch water cress*
> 3 *cups clear chicken broth*
> 1 *teaspoon salt*
> 1 *tablespoon dry sherry*
> *dash white pepper*

PREPARATION

Remove fish balls from the can and cut into halves.

Rinse under cold water and drain. Add 1 tablespoon sherry and set aside until ready for use.

Wash and clean the water cress. Break into 2″ pieces.

COOKING PROCEDURES

Bring the chicken broth to boil and add salt.

Add fish balls and water cress. As soon as mixture boils again, it is ready to be served. Sprinkle pepper to taste on top.

TIPS

Scandinavian fish balls are available in cans from fancy food stores, and are the closest thing to Chinese fish balls. Use fish balls packed in bouillon *only;* do not use those packed in tomato sauce. Fish balls other than Scandinavian available in local markets may be substituted if they are packed as described above.

If you have the time and interest, you may want to make your own fish balls. Try this recipe:

> ½ *pound fillet of flounder*
> 2 *scallions, finely chopped*
> 2 *slices fresh ginger root, minced*
> 1 *egg white*
> 2 *tablespoons cornstarch*
> ½ *teaspoon salt*

Remove from fillet any bones that still remain. Cut into ½″ cubes. Soak the minced ginger and chopped scallion in 1 cup water for 20 minutes. Strain the water and add to it ½ teaspoon salt. Blend the fish with the salted water in an electric blender for 2 minutes. Pour into bowl and carefully mix in the egg white and the 2 tablespoons cornstarch. Heat 4 cups of water slowly in a saucepan, dropping in mixture, one spoonful at a time, as the water heats. After about a minute the fish balls will float to the surface; when this happens, they are done. Put them in a large bowl of cold water and remove when you are ready to add them to the soup. Fish balls kept in cold water as above will stay fresh in the refrigerator for several days.

- ### FLANK STEAK IN OYSTER SAUCE
  TIME: 30 MINUTES

INGREDIENTS

12 *ounces flank steak*
8 *water chestnuts*
3 *tablespoons bottled oyster sauce*
1 *tablespoon dry sherry*
½ *teaspoon sugar*
2 *tablespoons peanut or corn oil*
2 *teaspoons cornstarch*

PREPARATION

Cut flank steak into long, 1″-wide strips and freeze for about 4 hours.

Slice steak against the grain about ⅛″ thick.

Slice water chestnuts into ¼″ pieces.

Mix the 3 tablespoons oyster sauce, 1 tablespoon sherry, ½ teaspoon sugar and 2 teaspoons cornstarch in a bowl and set aside.

COOKING PROCEDURES

Heat the 2 tablespoons oil in a wok or a heavy frying pan for about 2 minutes over a high flame.

Add the steak slices and stir immediately; continue to stir until oil covers all the surfaces and the meat turns a whitish color.

Add water chestnuts and mix well.

Stir in the sauce mixture; it will thicken gradually. When the steak is thoroughly mixed with the sauce, serve at once.

TIPS

The steak should be frozen before slicing so that it will be firm enough to cut into thin, neat slices.

Once a can of water chestnuts is opened, they should be removed from the can and rinsed under the cold-water faucet. Then they can be stored in a jar of cold water and left in the refrigerator for about 2 weeks, provided the water is changed every other day. Slices of water chestnut are pleasing additions to both fruit and vegetable salads. No cooking is necessary.

Oyster sauce is made of oyster extracts, water, salt and cornstarch. It comes in a bottle and can be kept for a long time on the cabinet shelf. Oyster sauce can be used as a cocktail dip as well as in cooked dishes.

Both water chestnuts and oyster sauce can be purchased in Chinese food stores or ordered by mail from some of the firms listed on pages 39–40.

● *CHICKEN–MUNG BEAN SPROUT SALAD*
TIME: 15 MINUTES

INGREDIENTS

> 1 *can bean sprouts or*
>   ½ *pound fresh bean sprouts*
> 1 *chicken breast*
> 1 *tablespoon soy sauce*
> 2 *teaspoons wine vinegar*
> 1 *teaspoon peanut or corn oil*
> 1 *teaspoon sesame-seed oil*
> ½ *teaspoon salt*
> ½ *teaspoon sugar*
> ¼ *teaspoon monosodium glutamate*

PREPARATION

If canned bean sprouts are used, drain and soak sprouts in cold water overnight. Drain again before using. If fresh bean sprouts are used, wash and clean, then pour plenty of boiling water over the sprouts to cook them slightly without actually boiling them. Drain and cool.

Boil the chicken breast in 2 cups of water for 10 minutes. Cool. Shred the chicken with your hand, discarding the skin and bone.

Mix the tablespoon of soy sauce, 2 teaspoons vinegar, 1 teaspoon peanut oil, 1 teaspoon sesame-seed oil, ½ teaspoon salt, ½ teaspoon sugar and ¼ teaspoon monosodium glutamate in a bowl.

Pour the sauce over the bean sprouts and mix thoroughly with chopsticks.

Mix in the chicken shreds. Serve cold.

TIPS

Fresh bean sprouts are preferable to canned, as they have better taste and texture. Bean sprouts can be grown in your own kitchen without too much difficulty. Directions are on pages 37–38.

Mung beans, more commonly known as green beans, are available in Chinese food stores. They resemble tiny peas in appearance.

This simple but tasty salad can be easily varied by using Julienne strips of boiled ham, canned or boiled shrimps, halved, shredded turkey breast or shredded roast beef to substitute for the chicken breast. The salad can be as simple or as fancy as the cook's imagination will allow.

Monosodium glutamate enhances the flavor of any dish, but again we emphasize that it should not be overused. When the quantity of a recipe is doubled, it is *not* necessary to double the amount of monosodium glutamate. Do not use more than ½ teaspoon for any one dish. There are many brands in the market; the most commonly available is Ac'cent.

• PORK SHREDS WITH DRIED BEAN CURD AND MUSHROOMS
TIME: 40 MINUTES

INGREDIENTS

> 2 medium-sized pork chops
> 4 ounces dried bean curd
> 4 medium-sized dried Chinese mushrooms
> 2 tablespoons peanut or corn oil
> 1 tablespoon soy sauce
> 1 teaspoon salt
> 1 teaspoon sugar
> 1 tablespoon dry sherry

PREPARATION

Cut the pork into thin strips and discard bones.

Soak the dried bean curd in warm water for 20 minutes. Drain and cut into strips.

Soak the mushrooms in warm water for 20 minutes. Cut into strips.

COOKING PROCEDURES

Heat the oil in a frying pan over a high flame. Add the pork strips and stir continuously for about 2 minutes.

Add 1 tablespoon sherry, 1 tablespoon soy sauce, 1 teaspoon salt and 1 teaspoon sugar. Mix well.

Add mushroom and bean-curd strips. Stir until all is mixed thoroughly.

Add ½ cup cold water, cover, turn flame to medium and cook for about 10 minutes more. Serve warm.

TIPS

Dried mushrooms and bean curd may be obtained at Chinese food stores or by mail order (see pages 39–40). Dried bean curd can be kept for 2 or 3 months. If kept longer it may turn rancid. It is sometimes called "second bamboo," as it is the second layer to be skimmed off in the making of bean curd. It is then dried and prepared for commercial use. It comes in pound and half-pound packages. When you buy it be sure to ask for the *second layer* as there are three layers in all, which are used in different ways by Chinese cooks.

Chinese dried mushrooms should be kept in a closed jar, where they will stay fresh for several months. If a clove of garlic is added to the jar it will keep away those tiny insects that sometimes appear in these mushrooms and destroy their meaty parts. Even after mushrooms are soaked in water, they will keep for several days in the refrigerator. Chinese mushrooms are similar to dried Hungarian and Italian mushrooms. They are slightly meatier and their flavor is not so strong. If European mushrooms are substituted, use a slightly smaller quantity than called for in the recipe.

- *ALMOND FLOAT*
  8 SERVINGS

INGREDIENTS

> ¾ cup (1 small can) undiluted evaporated milk
> 1 envelope unflavored gelatin
> 1¼ cups cold water
> 1 small can mandarin oranges
> 8 maraschino cherries
> 6 tablespoons sugar
> 1 tablespoon almond extract

PREPARATION

> Drain and save juice from mandarin oranges.
> Dissolve the gelatin in 3 tablespoons water.

COOKING PROCEDURES

> Heat the ¾ cup evaporated milk, the 1¼ cups water and the 6 tablespoons sugar to just below boiling.
> Add the dissolved gelatin to the milk and stir until completely mixed.
> Cool. Add almond extract.

Pour into a rectangular glass pan and keep in refrigerator until it sets, preferably overnight.

Cut into diamond-shaped pieces and float in syrup (see below) with oranges and cherries.

COOKING PROCEDURES FOR SYRUP

Dissolve ¼ cup sugar in 2 cups warm water. Cool. Add 1 teaspoon almond extract and the juice of the mandarin oranges. Use about ¼ cup for each serving.

TIPS

Almond Float is light and refreshing, and it may be served at any meal. If desired, pineapples, peaches, pears or fruit cocktail can be used instead of mandarin oranges, but the latter have a decidedly Oriental flavor.

This dessert can be made the day before. Leftovers can be kept in the refrigerator for several days.

MENU II
FOR 4 PERSONS

Chicken Velvet Corn Soup
Millionaire Chicken
Tan Chiao (Half-Moon Omelet) with Peas
Red Cabbage Salad
Boiled Rice (see page 66)
Tea
Lichee Delight

• CHICKEN VELVET CORN SOUP
TIME: 20 MINUTES

INGREDIENTS

> 1 *whole chicken breast, uncooked*
> 2 *egg whites*
> 1 *8-ounce can creamed corn*
> 3 *cups clear chicken broth*
> 1 *teaspoon dry sherry*
> 1 *teaspoon salt*
> 1 *tablespoon cornstarch*
> 2 *tablespoons minced cooked ham (optional)*

PREPARATION

Slice and mince the chicken breast, discarding the skin and bone.

Beat the egg whites until stiff and mix with the minced chicken.

Dissolve cornstarch in 2 tablespoons cold water.

COOKING PROCEDURES

Bring chicken broth to a boil; add 1 teaspoon salt.

Add creamed corn and let boil for 2 minutes.

Add pre-dissolved cornstarch, stirring continuously until soup is thickened.

Stir the chicken mixture into the soup. As soon as it boils again, the soup is ready.

Sprinkle the minced ham on top of the soup before serving.

TIPS

Minced ham can be made from boiled ham, sugar-cured baked ham or boiled Smithfield ham. Smithfield ham is considered the nearest in color, flavor and taste to the famous King Hwa ham of China, produced in King Hwa, Chekiang province.

Always prepare the soup last so that it will be hot and tasty. In China, soup is served along with rice and other dishes, not as a separate first course as is the custom in the West.

● *MILLIONAIRE CHICKEN*
TIME: 1 HOUR

INGREDIENTS

1 *chicken, 2 to 3 pounds*
1 *head lettuce*

INGREDIENTS FOR SAUCE, GROUP A:
4 *tablespoons soy sauce*
2 *tablespoons honey*
1 *clove crushed garlic*
½ *teaspoon salt*
¼ *teaspoon monosodium glutamate*

INGREDIENTS FOR SAUCE, GROUP B:
3 *tablespoons peanut or corn oil*
2 *scallions, chopped*
4 *slices fresh ginger root, minced*
½ *teaspoon Szechuen peppercorn, slightly crushed*
¼ *teaspoon crushed red pepper*

PREPARATION AND COOKING

Wash and clean the chicken.

Bring 3 quarts of water to boil in a large, deep pan.

Submerge the chicken in the boiling water and continue boiling for 15 minutes. Turn off the flame and let the chicken cool in the water for at least 20 minutes before taking it out.

Pull out as many large bones from the chicken as will come loose. Place the chicken in the refrigerator.

Wash and arrange the lettuce leaves on a large platter.

Cut chicken into 1″ x 2″ pieces and arrange over the lettuce.

Pour the warm sauce (see below) over the chicken and serve.

PREPARATION OF SAUCE

Combine the ingredients of Group A in a bowl and let stand for at least 5 minutes.

In a small pan over a low flame heat the Group B ingredients for about 3 minutes. Then pour B into the bowl containing A. Mix well. The sauce is now ready to pour over the chicken.

TIPS

This dish can be prepared beforehand. The chicken can be cooked the day before, cut an hour or so before dinnertime, arranged over lettuce on the platter and left in the refrigerator. The two groups of ingredients for the sauce can be assembled and placed in a bowl and saucepan respectively. The final preparation takes but a few minutes. Since Millionaire Chicken is served cold, it is an especially good dish for summer days.

The original Chinese name is Odd Flavor Chicken, because it uses such a variety of ingredients. On one occasion when I was preparing it, one of my students exclaimed that it was worth a million dollars. With one accord my entire class decided that this dish should be known as "Millionaire Chicken"—henceforth and forevermore.

● TAN CHIAO (HALF-MOON OMELET) WITH PEAS

TIME: 30 MINUTES

INGREDIENTS

4 eggs
½ cup (¼ pound) ground pork
1 package frozen peas
1 tablespoon soy sauce
1 tablespoon dry sherry
1 teaspoon sugar
1 teaspoon salt
2 tablespoons peanut or corn oil

PREPARATION

Beat the 4 eggs thoroughly.

Thaw the frozen peas.

Mix the pork with 1 teaspoon sugar, 1 tablespoon sherry, 1 tablespoon soy sauce and ½ teaspoon salt.

Using a small frying pan, 4″ in diameter, brush a little oil onto the pan and heat over a low flame.

Add 1 tablespoon of egg and let it set slightly.

Put 1 teaspoon pork just off the center of the egg pancake. Fold it in half and press down gently over the edge. Turn pancake over and cook for a minute. Remove and set aside. Repeat this process until all the eggs are used up. Makes about 12-14 small omelets.

COOKING PROCEDURES

Heat the remaining oil in a frying pan over a high flame. Add peas and stir fry for a minute.

Add ½ teaspoon salt and mix well.

Lower flame to medium and arrange the omelets over the peas.

Add ½ cup cold water and bring to boil.

Cover and cook for 5 minutes. Arrange on a platter and serve hot.

TIPS

Tan Chiaos may also be stuffed with minced shrimps, minced fillet of fish or ground steak.

Tan Chiaos can be made beforehand and stored in the refrigerator overnight. Frozen, they will keep for several weeks. Before freezing, they should be steamed for 10 minutes and cooled.

● *RED CABBAGE SALAD*
  TIME: 20 MINUTES

INGREDIENTS

1 *pound red cabbage*
2 *tablespoons peanut or corn oil*
2 *tablespoons soy sauce*
2 *tablespoons wine vinegar*
1 *tablespoon brown sugar*
¼ *teaspoon monosodium glutamate*
1 *dried red pepper (optional)*

PREPARATION

Wash cabbage and cut into 1″ squares.

COOKING PROCEDURES

Heat 1 tablespoon oil in a frying pan over a high flame and stir fry the cabbage. Remove from flame as soon as all the pieces of cabbage are coated with oil. Put cabbage into mixing bowl.

In the same frying pan, heat the remaining tablespoon of oil, 2 tablespoons soy sauce, 2 tablespoons wine vinegar, 1 tablespoon brown sugar, ¼ teaspoon monosodium glutamate and the dried red pepper. When this mixture begins to boil, pour it over the red cabbage. Stir well.

Weigh it down with a dish of water and store overnight in the refrigerator so that cabbage will absorb flavor of other ingredients. Serve cold.

TIPS

It is important not to overcook cabbage so that it will retain its crunchiness. The red pepper gives a slight peppery taste to this dish, but should not be eaten alone because—well, it's very peppery!

● *LICHEE DELIGHT*
TIME: 30 MINUTES

INGREDIENTS

½ *can lichees*
1 *small can sliced peaches*
red and green preserved cherries
4 *tablespoons sugar*
1 *package unflavored gelatin*

PREPARATION

Drain lichees and peaches, saving the juice.

In small custard cups, arrange red and green cherries, lichees and sliced peaches. Use about 3 lichees and 3 slices of peach in each cup.

COOKING PROCEDURES

Heat the juices with 4 tablespoons sugar and enough water to make 2 cups of liquid.

Dissolve the gelatin and add to the hot syrup. Mix thoroughly.

Fill each cup with syrup.

Chill in the refrigerator for several hours until set.

Before serving, place each cup in very hot water for a minute and turn out onto dessert plate to unmold. Makes about 4 or 5 servings.

TIPS

Lichees are a fruit canned in syrup and imported from Hong Kong. They can be purchased or mail-ordered from Chinese food stores (see pages 39–40 for partial listing). Each can of lichees will make 8 to 10 servings. After the can is opened, the lichees can be kept for several days.

For a larger quantity of Lichee Delight, use the whole can of lichees, double the quantity of peaches and cherries, use 2 packages of gelatin and double the quantity of liquid. Pineapple tidbits, mandarin oranges or sliced bananas can be used in place of peaches.

MENU III
FOR 4 PERSONS

Cellophane Noodle and Meat Ball Soup
Shrimps in Lobster Sauce
Agar-Agar Ham Salad
Chicken with Nuts in Hoisin Sauce
Boiled Rice (see page 66)
Tea
Golden Surprise (Sweet Filled Wontons)

- ### CELLOPHANE NOODLE AND
  MEAT BALL SOUP
  TIME: 30 MINUTES

INGREDIENTS

½ cup (¼ pound) ground pork
1 ounce dried cellophane noodles
3 cups chicken broth
1 scallion
1 tablespoon soy sauce
1 tablespoon dry sherry
1 teaspoon salt
¼ teaspoon monosodium glutamate

PREPARATION

Mix the pork with 1 tablespoon soy sauce and 1 tablespoon sherry. Make into 8 balls.

Soak the dried cellophane noodles in warm water for 20 minutes. With a pair of scissors cut noodles into 2″ lengths. Drain.

Wash and chop the scallion.

COOKING PROCEDURES

Heat about 1 quart water in a saucepan. When water boils, drop the meat balls in gently, one by one. Cook for 5 minutes. Put them in a dish and discard the water.

Heat the chicken broth in a saucepan with 1 teaspoon salt and ¼ teaspoon monosodium glutamate.

Add the cooked meat balls and the drained cellophane noodles and cook for 5 minutes.

Sprinkle chopped scallion over soup before serving.

TIPS

Ground steak may be substituted for pork in meat balls.

Cellophane noodles (so named because they appear almost transparent) are made from mung bean flour.

The noodles can be purchased or mail-ordered in half-pound and pound packages from Chinese food stores (see pages 39–40 for partial listing). They will keep on the cabinet shelf for a long time. If cellophane noodles are not available, egg noodles may be substituted.

● *SHRIMPS IN LOBSTER SAUCE*
Time: 40 Minutes

INGREDIENTS

1 *pound fresh uncooked shrimps*
½ *cup (¼ pound) ground pork*
2 *eggs*
2 *teaspoons fermented black beans*
2 *cloves garlic*
2 *scallions*
2 *tablespoons peanut or corn oil*
1 *tablespoon soy sauce*
1 *tablespoon dry sherry*
½ *teaspoon salt*
½ *teaspoon sugar*
1 *tablespoon cornstarch*

PREPARATION

Shell and devein the shrimps. Wash and drain. Beat the eggs.

Crush the black beans and the garlic with the side of a Chinese cleaver.

Wash scallions and cut into 2″ pieces.

Dissolve tablespoon of cornstarch in 2 tablespoons water.

COOKING PROCEDURES

Heat 2 tablespoons oil in a frying pan over a high flame. Add the black beans and the garlic. Stir a few times.

Add pork and continue stirring until the pork turns white, about 3 minutes.

Add shrimps and stir until they turn pink.

Add 1 tablespoon sherry, 1 tablespoon soy sauce, ½ teaspoon salt and ½ teaspoon sugar. Mix well.

Add scallion. Mix again.

Add ½ cup water. Bring to boil. Cover and cook over medium flame for 3 minutes.

Add the pre-dissolved cornstarch and stir slowly until it thickens.

Stir in the eggs. Turn off flame immediately and serve.

TIPS

Make certain that pork is well cooked over a high flame.

When making the sauce, it is important that the flame be turned off immediately after the beaten eggs have been added. This is necessary if you want to achieve a smooth, flowing sauce. It is called "lobster sauce" not because it contains lobster meat or juice—it doesn't—but because it is one of the sauces used to cook lobster. It is especially good when served very hot with boiled rice.

The fermented black beans can be purchased from Chinese food stores (see pages 39–40). Stored in a jar they will keep for a long time.

• AGAR-AGAR HAM SALAD

TIME: 10 MINUTES

INGREDIENTS

    1 *ounce agar-agar*
    4 *slices boiled ham*
    1 *tablespoon soy sauce*
    1 *teaspoon sesame-seed oil*
    1 *tablespoon sesame seeds (optional)*
    ½ *teaspoon salt*
    ½ *teaspoon sugar*
    ¼ *teaspoon monosodium glutamate*

PREPARATION

Soak the agar-agar in cold water for 5 minutes. Drain. Cut into 2″ pieces.

Cut the boiled ham into Julienne strips.

In a bowl mix 1 tablespoon soy sauce, 1 teaspoon sesame-seed oil, ½ teaspoon salt, ½ teaspoon sugar and ¼ teaspoon monosodium glutamate.

Pour this dressing into the agar-agar and mix thoroughly.

Put onto a plate and top with ham strips and sesame seeds. Serve cold.

Tips

Agar-agar is a seaweed product which looks like thin transparent noodles. For this salad it must be soaked in cold water *only*. If soaked in hot water it will dissolve and form a jellylike liquid. The Chinese use agar-agar as a coagulating agent in the same way that Americans use unflavored gelatin. It can be purchased or mail-ordered from Chinese food stores (see pages 39–40 for partial listing). It keeps for a long time.

This easily prepared salad can be varied by using shreds of chicken, roast beef or other cold meat instead of ham.

• CHICKEN WITH NUTS IN HOISIN SAUCE
Time: 30 Minutes

Ingredients

1 *whole chicken breast, uncooked*
6 *water chestnuts*
2 *medium-sized dried Chinese mushrooms*
½ *cup bamboo shoots*
½ *cup nuts (pecans, cashews or almonds)*
1 *tablespoon dry sherry*
1 *teaspoon cornstarch*
2 *tablespoons Hoisin sauce*
2 *tablespoons peanut or corn oil*

PREPARATION

Cut raw chicken breast into 1″ cubes. Discard bones and skin. Marinate in 1 tablespoon sherry and 1 teaspoon cornstarch for 10 minutes.

Dice the water chestnuts.

Soak mushrooms in warm water for about 20 minutes. Cut same size as water chestnuts.

Cut bamboo shoots into 1″ pieces.

COOKING PROCEDURES

Heat 2 tablespoons oil in a frying pan over a high flame.

Add the chicken and stir for about 2 minutes, or until chicken turns white. Be sure to stir continuously so that chicken will not stick to the pan.

Add mushrooms, bamboo shoots and water chestnuts and stir for another minute.

Add 2 tablespoons Hoisin sauce and mix well. Just before serving, add nuts to the mixture and stir a few times.

TIPS

Hoisin sauce, which is made from soybeans, salt, flour, sugar and food coloring, is packed in cans and may be purchased or mail-ordered from Chinese food stores (see pages 39–40 for partial listing). Once the can is opened, pour sauce into a jar and keep covered in the refrigerator. It will keep for months. If mixed with either tomato or chili sauce it can be used as a dip for plain cooked meat, chicken or shrimps.

Besides cashews, pecans and almonds, walnuts and peanuts are also good with this dish. If almonds or other nuts are large, halve them.

- ### GOLDEN SURPRISE
  ### (SWEET FILLED WONTONS)

INGREDIENTS FOR WRAPPING

> 1 *cup flour*
> ¼ *cup cold water*

PREPARATION OF WRAPPING

> Sift flour in bowl.
>
> Add ¼ cup cold water and knead. The dough should be as stiff and dry as possible.
>
> Cover dough with a wet cloth and let stand for 30 minutes to insure smoothness.
>
> Roll the dough out paper thin.
>
> Cut into 3″ x 3″ squares.

INGREDIENTS FOR FILLING

> 1 *8-ounce package pitted dates*
> 2 *tablespoons sesame seeds*
> ½ *cup dark corn syrup*

PREPARATION OF FILLING

> Grind dates together with sesame seeds and moisten with syrup.

PREPARATION OF WONTONS

> Use ½ teaspoon of filling for each wonton and follow directions on pages 52–53.

COOKING PROCEDURES

> Deep fry the wontons in oil at 375 degrees until golden brown. Remove to paper towels and cool slightly. Sprinkle with confectioners' sugar. Serve cool.

TIPS

> Golden Surprise can be kept for several weeks in a can with a tight lid.
>
> Wonton wrapping can be purchased at Chinese food stores (see pages 39–40). Some Chinese restaurants also sell them. Buy them if they are available, as they are tedious to make. Wonton wrappings may be frozen for future use.

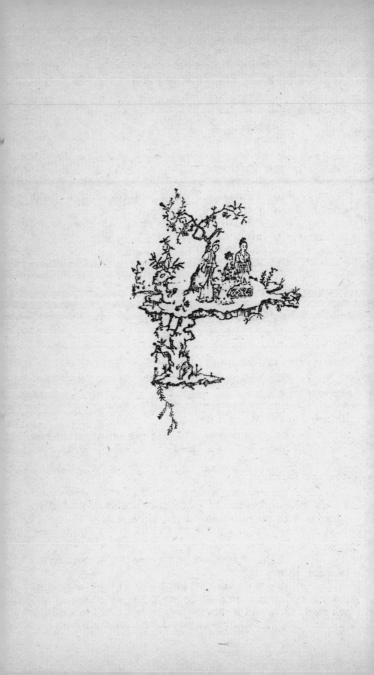

MENU IV
FOR 4 PERSONS

Cucumber-Pork Slice Soup
Roast Pork
Asparagus Salad
Steamed Fish
Boiled Rice (see page 66)
Tea
Individual Eight Precious Pudding

• CUCUMBER-PORK SLICE SOUP
Time: 25 Minutes

Ingredients

2 *medium-sized pork chops*
2 *cucumbers*
4 *cups meat stock*
1 *teaspoon salt*
¼ *teaspoon monosodium glutamate*

Preparation

Peel and cut the cucumbers into halves, lengthwise. Remove seeds. Cut into ¼" slices.

Remove bones and excess fat from pork chops. Slice meat into strips about 1" x ½" x ¼". Use bones to enrich stock if desired.

Cooking Procedures

Add salt to stock and bring to a boil. Add sliced pork and cook for 8 minutes.

Add cucumber slices and bring to boil again. Add monosodium glutamate and stir a few times. Serve hot.

Tips

Pork slices will be thoroughly cooked after boiling in the soup for 8 minutes.

Cook cucumbers briefly. As soon as they are transparent, the soup is ready.

Slices of shrimp, fish fillet or steak can be substituted for pork. For all of these the cooking time should be decreased to about 5 minutes.

• ROAST PORK

TIME: 3 *hours, including*
2 *hours for marinating*

INGREDIENTS

1 *pound lean pork*
4 *slices fresh ginger root*
1 *scallion*
2 *cloves garlic*
1 *tablespoon chili sauce*
1 *tablespoon Hoisin sauce*
4 *tablespoons dry sherry*
2 *tablespoons soy sauce*
½ *teaspoon salt*
2 *tablespoons honey*

PREPARATION

Cut pork into 1″ x 1″ x 4″ strips.

Wash scallion and cut into 2″ pieces.

Gently crush the 2 cloves of garlic with the flat side of the cleaver.

In a flat pan, mix the 4 slices of ginger root, the scallion, garlic, 1 tablespoon chili sauce, 1 tablespoon Hoisin sauce, 4 tablespoons sherry, 2 tablespoons soy sauce, 1 tablespoon honey and ½ teaspoon salt.

Marinate the pork in this mixture for 2 hours, turning over once after an hour. Remove pork from marinade and brush with remainder of honey.

Hook the pork strips over the railings in the oven (see pages 57–58).

Put 4 cups water in a large pan and place beneath the pork. This will catch the drippings and keep the pork strips moist.

COOKING PROCEDURES

Roast for 35 minutes at 350 degrees, then for 15 minutes at 450 degrees. Cool and slice.

TIPS

The best pork for roasting is pork tenderloin, but any cut of pork may be used if it is not too fat.

Roast pork can be served in many ways. Besides using it as a main dish, you can shred, dice, or cut it into chunks for combining with various vegetables. Just remember to add the roast pork at the very last, as it is already cooked and further cooking will cause loss of flavor. If roast pork is frozen it will keep for several weeks.

● ASPARAGUS SALAD
TIME: 10 MINUTES

INGREDIENTS

> 1 *package frozen asparagus spears*
> 2 *tablespoons soy sauce*
> 2 *teaspoons sesame-seed oil*
> 1 *teaspoon minced red preserved ginger*
> 1 *teaspoon sugar*
> ¼ *teaspoon monosodium glutamate*
> 6 *drops hot sauce (optional)*

PREPARATION

Thaw the asparagus spears slightly and cut into oblique pieces about 1" long (see page 18). Rinse with boiling water to cook slightly without actually parboiling. Drain.

Mix in a bowl the 2 tablespoons soy sauce, 2 teaspoons sesame-seed oil, 1 teaspoon sugar and ¼ teaspoon monosodium glutamate.

Combine dressing with asparagus. Add hot sauce and mix again.

Top with minced red ginger.

TIPS

If fresh asparagus is in season, by all means use it instead of the frozen. Clean and then cut as frozen asparagus. Parboil and cool; then proceed as above.

Red ginger preserved in syrup comes in a jar and may be purchased from Chinese food stores (see pages 39–40 for partial listing). It is used for color as well as flavor. Combined with green asparagus, it makes an appropriate Christmas salad.

- **STEAMED SEA BASS**
  TIME: 30 MINUTES

INGREDIENTS

> 1 *sea bass, about 1½ pounds*
> ½ *teaspoon shredded fresh ginger root*
> 1 *scallion cut in 2" pieces*
> ½ *teaspoon fermented black beans*
> 1 *tablespoon soy sauce*
> 1 *tablespoon dry sherry*
> 1 *tablespoon peanut or corn oil*

PREPARATION

Clean and wash the sea bass. Dry inside and outside.

Put the *whole* fish into a heatproof dish.

Mix ½ teaspoon shredded fresh ginger root, ½ teaspoon black beans, 1 tablespoon soy sauce, 1 tablespoon sherry, 1 tablespoon oil, and the scallion. Pour all over fish.

Heat 2 quarts water until boiling in a large (8-quart) saucepan.

COOKING PROCEDURES

Place a rack in the saucepan and put the dish containing the bass on it. Be sure the water is even with the rack and not higher, so that the water, when it boils again, will not get into the dish.

Cover tightly and steam the fish for 15 minutes over a high flame. Serve immediately.

TIPS

To serve Chinese style the fish must be brought to the table whole, including the head. If you prefer, however, remove the head before steaming the fish.

Fish must be absolutely fresh for steaming. Fine-textured fish such as porgy, trout, butterfish, flounder, sole and whitefish can all be steamed in the same manner as sea bass. Fillets of any of the above fish can be steamed the same way and are easier to handle because they are smaller.

Fermented black beans can be purchased at Chinese food stores (see pages 39–40 for partial listing). If you do not use the beans, substitute ½ teaspoon salt.

●   *INDIVIDUAL EIGHT PRECIOUS PUDDING*
      TIME: 1½ HOURS

INGREDIENTS

    1 *cup glutinous rice*
    2 *tablespoons sugar*
    1 *tablespoon shortening*
    4 *tablespoons red bean paste*
    red and green pine-ettes (*preserved pineapple bits*)

PREPARATION

Wash the rice. Drain.

Cook in 1¼ cups of water, following directions on page 66 for boiled rice.

When rice is cool enough to touch, mix in the sugar and shortening.

Grease 4 custard cups with a little shortening and arrange the red and green pine-ettes at the bottom of each cup.

Fill each cup ⅓ full of rice. Press down firmly so that when turning out pudding it will hold its shape.

Add 1 tablespoon red bean paste to each cup and smooth it over the rice. Cover with another ⅓ cup of rice. Be sure all bean paste is covered. If it is not, the bean paste will be diluted during steaming, run into the rest of the pudding and ruin its appearance.

COOKING PROCEDURES

In a steamer or on a high rack, steam the pudding, using plenty of water, for 30 minutes. (The top layer of rice will absorb the steam.)

While still hot, unmold on dessert plates and top each pudding with warm sugar water.

To make sugar water:

Bring to boil 1 cup water with 4 tablespoons sugar, stirring to dissolve the sugar. Remove from heat. Add 1 teaspoon almond extract. Use about 4 tablespoons for each serving.

TIPS

This is called Eight Precious Pudding because in China we use eight different dried fruits to make a design at the bottom of the plate. Among these dried ingredients may be lotus seeds, black jujube, green and red plums, dragon eye, white meat of watermelon seeds and others. The pudding is usually made in a large round dish, from which the whole family is served. This is not as neat as individual cups, nor is it as easy to reheat. The individual puddings can be made and steamed the day before. To reheat, steam again for 10 minutes. Melon balls or red and green cherries may be used instead of pine-ettes. But pine-ettes (available in fancy food stores) are a little more tasty.

Red bean paste, canned, is sold at Chinese food stores (see pages 39–40 for partial listing). If not available, date or coconut filling may be substituted.

MENU V
FOR 4 PERSONS

Chinese Mustard Green and Bean Curd Soup
Five Diced Fish
Mo-Shu-Ro, Pork Dish
Cucumber Salad
Boiled Rice (see page 66)
Tea
Assorted Chinese Fruits

• CHINESE MUSTARD GREEN AND BEAN CURD SOUP
Time: 15 Minutes

Ingredients

> ½ pound Chinese mustard greens
> 1 square fresh bean curd, about 3" x 3"
> 4 cups clear chicken broth
> 1 teaspoon salt

Preparation

Wash and cut the mustard greens into 1" pieces.
Cut the bean curd in half and then slice into ½" pieces.

Cooking Procedures

Bring to boil 4 cups clear chicken broth and add salt.
Add the bean curd and mustard greens and boil for 10 minutes without cover. Serve hot.

Tips

If fresh bean curd is not available, canned bean curd can be substituted. Bean curd is made from soybeans and has a high protein content. The soup should be cooked without a cover so that the mustard greens will retain their color.

• FIVE DICED FISH
Time: 30 Minutes

Ingredients

> 1 2-pound sea bass, whole
> ¼ cup fresh peas
> ¼ cup diced carrots
> ¼ cup diced water chestnuts
> 2 tablespoons diced ham

2 *tablespoons diced Chinese mushrooms*
1 *tablespoon plus 1 teaspoon salt*
½ *teaspoon sugar*
¼ *teaspoon monosodium glutamate*
2 *tablespoons cornstarch*
1 *cup cold water*

PREPARATION

Clean the sea bass, leaving it whole.

Rub the fish with 1 tablespoon salt inside and outside. Let it stand for 5 minutes.

Place the diced carrots peas, mushrooms and water chestnuts in ½ cup of water. Bring to boil and cook for 3 minutes. Drain.

COOKING PROCEDURES

Bring to boil 2 quarts water in a large saucepan.

Submerge the fish in the boiling water, bending it to fit pan if necessary. Bring to boil again. Let it boil for 4 minutes. Turn off flame. Leave fish in hot water for at least 10 minutes.

Dissolve 2 tablespoons cornstarch in 1 cup water; bring to boil while stirring, until it thickens. Add 1 teaspoon salt, ½ teaspoon sugar, ¼ teaspoon monosodium glutamate. Mix well.

Add the carrots, peas, mushrooms and water chestnuts, mix, and then add ham.

Remove fish from liquid, put it on a platter, and pour sauce over the fish. Serve immediately.

TIPS

The fish must be really fresh for this dish. Other fish of similar size may be substituted for sea bass.

Chinese mushrooms must be soaked in warm water for 20 minutes before you dice them.

- ### MO-SHU-RO, PORK DISH
  TIME: 30 MINUTES

INGREDIENTS

½ cup lean shredded pork
½ cup fresh bean sprouts
10 dried golden needles (tiger-lily buds)
1 tablespoon dried Chinese fungi ("tree ears")
2 medium-sized Chinese mushrooms
2 eggs
2 tablespoons peanut or corn oil
2 tablespoons soy sauce
1 teaspoon sugar
¼ teaspoon monosodium glutamate

PREPARATION

Wash and drain the bean sprouts.

Soak golden needles, fungi and mushrooms together in 1 cup warm water for 20 minutes. Wash and drain.

Shred the mushrooms.

Beat the eggs and scramble in 1 tablespoon oil.

COOKING PROCEDURES

Heat remaining oil over high flame in a wok or a regular frying pan.

Add shredded pork and stir for about 2 minutes.

Add 2 tablespoons soy sauce, 1 teaspoon sugar and ¼ teaspoon monosodium glutamate and stir a few more times.

Add golden needles, fungi and mushroom shreds, and mix well.

Add 2 tablespoons water and bring to boil.

Add scrambled eggs and bean sprouts and mix thoroughly. Serve hot.

TIPS

This is a typical northern dish. The preparation takes a little time but the cooking is very quick. It can be kept frozen for a few days and then reheated. The golden needles (dried tiger-lily buds) and the "tree ears" can be purchased or mail-ordered from Chinese food stores (see pages 39–40). They are very light in weight, and a few ounces will last a long time. They can be kept in jars on the cabinet shelf.

• CUCUMBER SALAD
TIME: 25 MINUTES

INGREDIENTS

1 *medium-sized cucumber*
1 *tablespoon wine vinegar*
1 *tablespoon soy sauce*
1 *tablespoon sugar*
1 *teaspoon sesame-seed oil*
¼ *teaspoon monosodium glutamate*
½ *teaspoon salt*

PREPARATION

Peel the cucumber. Cut into very thin slices. Sprinkle with ½ teaspoon salt and let stand for about 20 minutes. Drain.

Mix in a bowl 1 tablespoon vinegar, 1 tablespoon soy sauce, 1 tablespoon sugar, 1 teaspoon sesame-seed oil and ¼ teaspoon monosodium glutamate.

Pour the sauce over the drained cucumber. Mix and serve cold.

TIPS

Be sure that the sauce is mixed with the cucumber at the last minute in order to keep the color of the cucumber light.

If sesame-seed oil is not available, use a teaspoon of any salad oil. But sesame-seed oil is the ingredient that makes the salad distinctive.

Lettuce leaves, spinach leaves or shredded celery cabbage can be used in place of cucumber to make variations of this salad.

● ASSORTED CHINESE FRUITS

INGREDIENTS

        10-12 *preserved kumquats*
        6 *slices preserved red ginger*
        1 *small can pineapple chunks*
        1 *small can mandarin oranges*
        6 *maraschino cherries*

PREPARATION

Drain the mandarin oranges and pineapple chunks. In a salad bowl filled with crushed ice arrange the kumquats, ginger, pineapple chunks and oranges. Decorate with maraschino cherries.

TIPS

Mandarin oranges in cans are available in most markets.

Kumquats can be preserved at home if fresh kumquats are in season (see page 87). Kumquats can be found in specialty food stores as well as Chinese food stores. Both preserved kumquats and preserved ginger keep for a long time and can conveniently be stored on the shelf. Canned lichee nuts, if available, are a delightful addition to assorted fruits.

MENU VI
FOR 4 PERSONS

Winter Melon and Ham Soup
Szechuen Pork
Ground Steak with Onions
Anchovy Lettuce Salad
Boiled Rice (see page 66)
Tea
Almond "Tea"

●   *WINTER MELON AND HAM SOUP*
TIME: 20 MINUTES

INGREDIENTS

> 1 *pound winter melon*
> ¼ *cup ham slices, 1" x 1" x ¼"*
> 4 *dried Chinese mushrooms*
> 4 *cups chicken broth*
> 1 *teaspoon salt*
> ¼ *teaspoon monosodium glutamate*

PREPARATION

Peel and wash the winter melon. Drain. Cut into 1" x 1" x ¼" slices.

Soak the dried mushrooms in ½ cup warm water for 20 minutes. Cut each into 2 to 4 pieces.

COOKING PROCEDURES

Add the melon slices to the broth and bring to boil over high flame.

Add mushrooms, salt and monosodium glutamate.

Cover and cook over medium flame for 10 minutes.

Add ham and bring to boil once more. Serve hot.

TIPS

Winter melon is very much like summer squash. It is a large green melon (as large as a basketball) with a frostlike outside layer. The seeds are found in the white spongy material in the center of the melon. Chinese grocery stores will cut winter melons into 1- or 2-pound pieces on request.

Boiled ham may be used for the ham slices, but the Chinese prefer Smithfield ham, which is nearest in texture and taste to the King Hwa ham produced in King Hwa, in Chekiang province. To keep ham for future use, clean away the skin and fat; wash, dry, and boil in water for 20 minutes. Store in the refrigerator and it will be ready for recipes calling for ham, whether it be sliced, shredded or minced.

● SZECHUEN PORK
TIME: 30 MINUTES

INGREDIENTS

1 *pound lean pork (any cut)*
½ *cup leek, cut in 2" pieces*
½ *cup bamboo shoots, sliced*
½ *cup vegetable steak*
½ *cup sweet pepper*
3 *tablespoons peanut or corn oil*
2 *cloves garlic*
2 *slices fresh ginger root*
4 *tablespoons Hoisin sauce*
1 *teaspoon sugar*
¼ *teaspoon crushed red pepper*

PREPARATION

Boil the entire piece of lean pork for 20 minutes. Cool thoroughly. Slice into pieces about 1" x 1" x ¼".

Cut sweet pepper and vegetable steak into similar-sized pieces.

COOKING PROCEDURES

Heat 3 tablespoons oil in a frying pan over a high flame and in it cook the garlic and ginger for 1 minute.

Add leek, bamboo shoots, sweet pepper and vegetable steak. Mix well. Mix in the crushed red pepper.

Add pork slices and stir a few times.

Add 2 tablespoons water and bring to boil. Add sugar and Hoisin sauce and stir quickly for about a minute, until the sauce coats all the ingredients. Serve with boiled rice.

TIPS

Szechuen cooking is usually peppery. The Chinese name of this dish is "Twice-Cooked Pork," because the pork is boiled, cooled and sliced before it is stir fried with all the other ingredients.

Vegetable steak, made of wheat gluten, is so called because it is the steak of vegetarians and it looks, in fact, just like a small steak. It is sold in cans at health-food stores.

● *GROUND STEAK WITH ONIONS*
TIME: 30 MINUTES

INGREDIENTS

½ *pound ground round steak*
½ *pound onions*
4-6 *water chestnuts*
3 *tablespoons peanut or corn oil*
3 *tablespoons soy sauce*
2 *tablespoons dry sherry*
1 *teaspoon sugar*
½ *teaspoon salt*
1 *tablespoon cornstarch*

PREPARATION

Mix the ground steak with 3 tablespoons soy sauce, 2 tablespoons sherry and 1 teaspoon sugar in a bowl.

Slice the onions.

Mince the water chestnuts.

COOKING PROCEDURES

Heat 1 tablespoon oil in a frying pan over high flame and stir fry the onion for 4 minutes. Add salt and mix well. Reserve in bowl.

Heat 2 tablespoons oil in the same frying pan and stir fry the steak. Stir continuously until all the steak turns a whitish color.

Add the onion and water chestnuts, lower flame to medium, cover and cook for 10 minutes.

Thicken with 1 tablespoon cornstarch pre-dissolved in 2 tablespoons cold water. Serve hot.

TIPS

This is a good luncheon dish. Use it to fill a rice ring. It can be prepared beforehand and reheated for later use.

• ANCHOVY LETTUCE SALAD
  TIME: 10 MINUTES

INGREDIENTS

2 cups shredded head lettuce
2 anchovies, minced
1 tablespoon wine vinegar
1 tablespoon soy sauce
1 teaspoon sugar
1 teaspoon sesame-seed oil
¼ teaspoon monosodium glutamate

PREPARATION

Mix 1 tablespoon vinegar, 1 tablespoon soy sauce, 1 teaspoon sugar, 1 teaspoon sesame-seed oil and ¼ teaspoon monosodium glutamate in a bowl.

Mix the minced anchovies with the lettuce.

Pour the sauce over the lettuce and mix well.

TIPS

Other greens of the lettuce family can be used in place of head lettuce. If sesame-seed oil is not available, use olive oil or any other salad oil.

• ALMOND "TEA"

INGREDIENTS

4 heaping tablespoons almond paste
3½ cups cold water

PREPARATION

Soak the almond paste in 3½ cups cold water for about 30 minutes. Sieve through a double layer of cheese-cloth.

COOKING PROCEDURES

Heat in a double boiler until very hot and serve.

TIPS

Almond paste does not require sugar to sweeten it. It comes in cans of various sizes and can be purchased in fancy grocery stores.

The Chinese call this almond beverage "tea" because it is drunk, as a tea, usually between the many courses of a banquet. If desired, this "tea" can be cooled and served as a cold drink.

MENU VII
FOR 4 PERSONS

Sour and Hot Soup
Lobster with Black Bean Sauce
String Beans in Special Bean-Curd Sauce
Cellophane Noodles with Pork Shreds
Boiled Rice (see page 66)
Tea
Date and Sesame Seed Ping

- ### SOUR AND HOT SOUP
  TIME: 20 MINUTES

INGREDIENTS

　　¼ cup pork shreds
　　¼ cup dried Chinese fungi (tree ears),
　　　　measured after soaking
　　¼ cup shredded bamboo shoots
　　2 medium-sized dried Chinese mushrooms
　　6 to 8 dried tiger-lily buds (golden needles)
　　½ cake fresh bean curd
　　1 egg
　　4 cups chicken broth
　　1 teaspoon soy sauce
　　½ teaspoon sugar
　　1 teaspoon salt
　　2 tablespoons wine vinegar
　　1 teaspoon sesame-seed oil
　　¼ teaspoon black pepper
　　¼ teaspoon monosodium glutamate
　　2 tablespoons cornstarch

PREPARATION

　　Soak the mushrooms and tiger-lily buds in ¼ cup warm water for 20 minutes. Drain. Shred mushrooms.

　　Cut the fresh bean curd into slices 1" x ¼" x ¼".

　　Beat the egg.

　　Dissolve the 2 tablespoons cornstarch in 3 tablespoons cold water.

COOKING PROCEDURES

　　In a saucepan bring to boil the chicken broth with pork shreds, bamboo shoots, fungi, mushroom shreds, tiger-lily buds and bean-curd slices, and boil for 10 minutes.

　　Add 1 teaspoon soy sauce, ½ teaspoon sugar, 1 teaspoon salt, 2 tablespoons vinegar, ¼ teaspoon pepper and ¼ teaspoon monosodium glutamate.

　　Thicken with the cornstarch. Turn off heat and immediately add the beaten eggs. Gently stir a few times.

Add 1 teaspoon sesame-seed oil just before serving to complete the exotic quality of the soup.

TIPS

Tree ears must always be soaked in warm water before using. The ¼ cup called for in this recipe is measured after the fungi are soaked. To measure before soaking, allow about 2 tablespoons.

The quantity of pepper and vinegar may be increased or decreased according to individual taste.

• LOBSTER WITH BLACK BEAN SAUCE
  TIME: 40 MINUTES

INGREDIENTS

1 *live lobster (about 2 pounds)*
¼ *cup ground pork (2 ounces)*
1 *egg*
1 *tablespoon fermented black beans*
2 *scallions*
2 *slices fresh ginger root*
1 *tablespoon dry sherry*
1 *tablespoon soy sauce*
½ *teaspoon salt*
½ *teaspoon sugar*
2 *tablespoons peanut or corn oil*
1 *tablespoon cornstarch*

PREPARATION

Wash lobster. Cut off the head at the groove in a semicircle. Chop off the claws and legs. Split the lobster lengthwise. Discard gills, intestinal canal and stomach. Cut the lobster meat (still in shell) into bite-sized pieces.

Crush the black beans with the flat side of a cleaver.

Beat the egg.

Wash scallions and cut into 2″ pieces.

Dissolve the tablespoon of cornstarch in 2 tablespoons cold water.

COOKING PROCEDURES

Heat 2 tablespoons oil in a frying pan over a high flame.

Add the black beans and ginger and stir for a minute.

Remove ginger and add ground pork; continue stirring for about 3 minutes.

Add lobster and stir until the lobster turns pink (about 2 minutes).

Add 1 tablespoon sherry, 1 tablespoon soy sauce, ½ teaspoon salt and ½ teaspoon sugar. Mix well.

Add ½ cup water. Bring to boil. Cover and cook over medium flame for 3 minutes.

Stir in cornstarch and keep stirring until mixture thickens.

Add scallions and stir a few times.

Pour in the egg gently and turn off heat. Stir again. Serve hot.

TIPS

The pork should be well cooked over a high flame.

Garlic may be added for those who like it. Ginger root may be omitted if garlic is used.

● *STRING BEANS IN*
SPECIAL BEAN-CURD SAUCE
TIME: 15 MINUTES

INGREDIENTS

12 *ounces fresh young string beans*
¼ *teaspoon sugar*
¼ *teaspoon salt*
1 *tablespoon special bean-curd sauce*
2 *tablespoons peanut or corn oil*

PREPARATION

Break the string beans into 2″ pieces. Wash and drain.

Mix the special bean-curd sauce with ¼ teaspoon sugar and ½ cup cold water in a bowl.

COOKING PROCEDURES

Heat 2 tablespoons oil in a frying pan and stir fry the string beans. Continue stirring until oil coats all the beans. Add ¼ teaspoon salt and mix well.

Add the prepared bean-curd sauce and mix a few times. After it begins to boil, turn heat to medium, cover and cook for 10 minutes. Serve warm.

TIPS

Special bean-curd sauce, known as *fu-jo*, is bean curd preserved in sherry and brine. The sauce is first steamed and then fermented before it is bottled. It may be purchased in Chinese food stores (see pages 39–40 for partial listing). Once the taste for this special bean-curd sauce is acquired, it adds zest to most vegetables and may be used in place of salt in cooking spinach, broccoli and other greens.

● *CELLOPHANE NOODLES WITH PORK SHREDS*
   TIME: 30 MINUTES

INGREDIENTS

    2 *medium-sized lean pork chops*
    4 *ounces cellophane noodles*
    3 *tablespoons peanut or corn oil*
    2 *tablespoons soy sauce*
    ½ *teaspoon salt*
    ½ *teaspoon sugar*
    ¼ *teaspoon monosodium glutamate*
    2 *scallions*
    1 *tablespoon sherry*

PREPARATION

Soak the cellophane noodles in warm water for 10 minutes. Drain and cut them into 2″ pieces. There should be about 2 cups after soaking.

Shred pork.

Wash scallions and cut into 2″ pieces.

COOKING PROCEDURES

Heat 1 tablespoon oil in a frying pan over high flame. Add pork and stir for 2 minutes until pork changes color.

Add 1 tablespoon sherry, 2 tablespoons soy sauce, ½ teaspoon sugar, ½ teaspoon salt and ¼ teaspoon monosodium glutamate. Mix thoroughly.

Add scallions and mix again. Remove all from pan and set aside.

Heat 2 tablespoons oil in same frying pan over high flame. Add cellophane noodles and stir a few times. Pour in prepared pork mixture and stir well.

Add ½ cup cold water, bring to boil, cover, then turn heat to medium and cook for about 5 minutes, or until all the water is absorbed. Serve hot.

TIPS

This recipe may be varied by using veal or beef instead of pork. Proceed in the same manner as above.

If this dish is cooked beforehand, to reheat add ¼ cup of cold water and heat over low flame until hot.

For another way to use cellophane noodles see page 110.

● DATE AND SESAME SEED PING
TIME: 40 MINUTES

INGREDIENTS

For wrapping:
1 *roll frozen biscuit dough*
2 *tablespoons sesame seeds*
2 *egg whites*

For filling:
1 8-ounce package pitted dates
2 tablespoons sesame seeds
½ cup dark corn syrup

PREPARATION

Grind dates with 2 tablespoons sesame seeds and moisten with syrup.

Divide filling into 20 portions of about 1 teaspoon each, and form into balls.

Divide roll of frozen dough into 10 pieces and cut each piece in half.

Put remaining 2 tablespoons sesame seeds into a small dish. Put egg whites into another small dish.

Roll dough out to circles about 1½″ in diameter.

Place a ball of filling in the center of each, pinch edges together and flatten slightly.

Dip one surface in the egg white and dip that same surface in sesame seeds.

With sesame-seed side up, arrange the 20 pings on a cooky sheet.

COOKING PROCEDURES

Preheat the oven to 350 degrees and bake the pings for 10 to 12 minutes. Serve either hot or cold.

TIPS

If preferred, piecrust mix can be used instead of frozen biscuit dough. Apricot or peach preserves can be used as filling in place of dates.

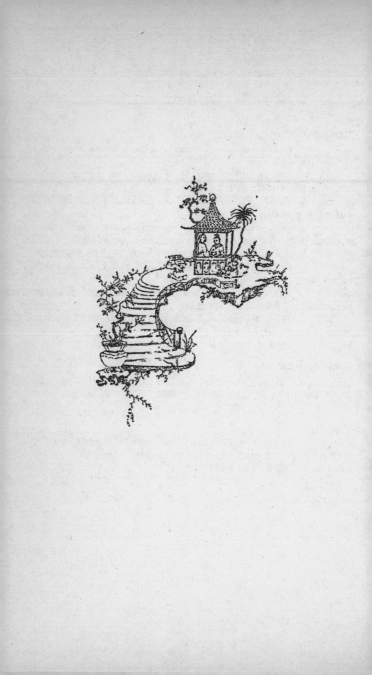

MENU VIII
FOR 4 PERSONS

Abalone and Chicken Soup
Sweet-Sour Fish
Cucumber Stuffed with Ground Pork
Chinese Greens with Bamboo Shoots and Mushrooms
Boiled Rice (see page 66)
Tea
Chinese Steamed Cake

• ABALONE AND CHICKEN SOUP
TIME: 10 MINUTES

INGREDIENTS

    ½ cup canned abalone, sliced
    ¼ cup boiled chicken breast, sliced
    ½ cup fresh mushrooms, sliced
    4 cups chicken broth
    ½ cup juice from canned abalone
    ½ teaspoon salt
    2 ounces snow peas (about 18-20 pods)
    ¼ cup boiled ham, sliced

PREPARATION

String the snow peas as you would string beans. Wash and parboil. Float in cold water until ready for use.

COOKING PROCEDURES

Heat the chicken broth with the abalone juice. Add salt.

Add fresh mushroom slices and bring to boil.

Add chicken, ham and abalone slices.

When soup begins to boil again, add snow peas. Serve hot.

TIPS

Abalone is a shellfish which is sold canned in the East. It is already cooked and ready to eat, so any additional cooking time must be brief. The juice is very tasty and should be used in the soup.

Sliced abalone can also be stir fried with water chestnuts, bamboo shoots, Chinese mushrooms and Chinese cabbage. It is important that these vegetables be stir fried first and the abalone added at the last minute. Otherwise the abalone will tend to be tough and rubbery.

- ### SWEET-SOUR FISH
  TIME: 25 MINUTES

INGREDIENTS

1 *sea bass (about 2 pounds)*
2 *scallions*
2 *slices fresh ginger root*
2 *tablespoons soy sauce*
3 *tablespoons wine vinegar*
3 *tablespoons sugar*
1 *teaspoon salt*
1 *tablespoon cornstarch*
oil for deep frying

PREPARATION

Wash and dry the sea bass inside and outside.

Make 3 or 4 diagonal cuts on each side of the bass so that added flavoring will be absorbed by the fish.

Rub both inside and outside of the bass with 1 teaspoon of salt and let stand for 10 minutes.

Wash scallions and cut into ¼″ pieces.

Mince the ginger.

Mix 2 tablespoons soy sauce, 3 tablespoons vinegar, 3 tablespoons sugar and 1 tablespoon cornstarch in ½ cup cold water.

COOKING PROCEDURES

Deep fry the fish for about 5-8 minutes or until golden brown. Place in a deep platter.

Stir fry the scallions and the ginger together in 1 tablespoon oil.

Add vinegar-soy sauce mixture and bring to boil.

Pour the mixture over the fish and serve hot.

TIPS

The sea bass must be very fresh. It should not weigh more than 2 pounds, as a larger fish is harder to cook this way.

Vary the amount of sugar and vinegar to taste.

● *CUCUMBER STUFFED WITH GROUND PORK*
TIME: 30 MINUTES

INGREDIENTS

> 2 *medium-sized cucumbers*
> ½ *cup ground pork (about ¼ pound)*
> 1 *slice fresh ginger root, minced*
> 1 *tablespoon dry sherry*
> 1 *tablespoon soy sauce*
> 1 *teaspoon salt*
> 1 *teaspoon sugar*
> ¼ *teaspoon monosodium glutamate*
> 1 *tablespoon peanut or corn oil*

PREPARATION

Peel the cucumbers and cut crosswise into 4 or 5 segments. Scoop the seeds from the center of each segment.

Mix the pork with 1 tablespoon sherry, 1 tablespoon soy sauce, 1 teaspoon sugar, ½ teaspoon salt and minced ginger Mix well.

Stuff each segment of the cucumber with the pork mixture.

COOKING PROCEDURES

Heat 1 tablespoon oil in a heavy frying pan over a high flame.

Stand each segment of cucumber in the pan so that a side with stuffing rests on the bottom of the pan. Brown quickly.

After about 2 minutes, flip each cucumber over and brown the other side for 2 more minutes.

Add ¼ cup cold water, bring to boil. Cover and cook for 2 minutes.

Add ½ teaspoon salt and ¼ teaspoon monosodium glutamate. Continue cooking with cover over medium flame for about 15 minutes. Serve hot.

TIPS

This dish can be prepared the day before and reheated in a casserole in the oven before serving.

If desired, minced shrimps, ground beef or veal can be substituted for the pork in the stuffing.

• CHINESE GREENS WITH BAMBOO SHOOTS
  AND MUSHROOMS
  TIME: 40 MINUTES

INGREDIENTS

1 *pound Chinese greens* (bok choy)
½ *cup bamboo shoots, sliced*
4 *medium-sized dried Chinese mushrooms*
1 *teaspoon salt*
¼ *teaspoon monosodium glutamate*
2 *tablespoons peanut or corn oil*

PREPARATION

Wash Chinese greens and cut into 1″ pieces.

Soak mushrooms in warm water for 20 minutes. Cut each mushroom into 4 pieces.

COOKING PROCEDURES

Heat 2 tablespoons oil in a frying pan over a high flame. Add 1 teaspoon salt.

Stir fry the greens for 3 to 4 minutes. Add mushrooms and bamboo slices. Mix well. Add ¼ teaspoon monosodium glutamate.

Add ¼ cup cold water; bring to boil. Cover, turn flame to medium and cook for 6 minutes. Mix a few more times. Serve hot.

If the greens are very tender and there is a great deal of liquid, cook over high flame without cover for 2 more minutes before serving.

TIPS

Chinese greens, also known as *bok choy*, can be purchased in Chinese food stores (see pages 39–40 for partial listing.)

● *CHINESE STEAMED CAKE*
  TIME: 1¼ HOURS

INGREDIENTS

2 *cups flour*
3 *eggs*
2 *tablespoons shortening*
1 *cup brown sugar*
1 *tablespoon baking powder*
¼ *cup chopped nuts*

PREPARATION

Sift 2 cups flour and 1 tablespoon baking powder together twice.

Cream 1 cup sugar with 2 tablespoons shortening. Add 3 eggs and mix well.

Add the sifted flour and stir for 2 minutes until thoroughly mixed.

Mix in the nuts.

Pour into greased heatproof dish 7″ in diameter.

COOKING PROCEDURES

Steam over boiling water, uncovered, for 1 hour. Cool and slice.

TIPS

The Chinese use lard as shortening, but any vegetable shortening may be substituted.

Chopped dates or dried fruits may be used in place of nuts.

4. GOURMET DISHES FOR CHINESE BANQUETS

FOOD FIT FOR A CHINESE GOURMET

*Bêche-de-Mer (Sea Cucumber) with Chicken and
    Meat Balls*
Bird's Nest Soup
Buddha's Delight
Chicken and Chinese Sausage Rice
Dried Fish Maw with Ham and Peas
Dried Scallops with Radish Balls
Gold Coin Mushrooms
Happy Family
Pork Shreds and Szechuen Preserved Kohlrabi
Shark's Fins with Chinese Cabbage
Shrimps, Szechuen Style
*Soochow Chiang (Pork, Mushrooms and Bamboo
    Shoots)*

Food Fit for a Chinese Gourmet

SHARK'S FIN and bird's nest soup, bear's paw and bêche-de-mer—these are among the most exotic of Chinese delicacies. Such dishes have two things in common: they are very difficult to prepare, and they usually appear only at that most elaborate of Chinese gatherings—the banquet.

It takes an abundance of skill and patience to produce Chinese gourmet dishes. Some actually require days of preparation under the supervision of expert chefs who have learned their trade after years of apprenticeship. To do justice to all this talent and effort, Chinese banquets are usually leisurely eating sessions, with one course following another in a seemingly endless procession. While a Chinese banquet is usually held to observe a birthday or a wedding, to honor a special guest or to celebrate a festival, the real center of attention at any banquet is the food and drink.

It would be pointless to mislead a beginner in Chinese cookery by implying that these Chinese gourmet dishes can be perfected after just one or two tries. Some of these recipes are admittedly tricky and require practice—and more practice—to perfect. Nevertheless, I have included them for two reasons. First, anyone with a real interest in Chinese cookery should have some idea of the highest expressions of the art of Chinese cooking. Secondly, these recipes will provide a real challenge to those who have mastered the basic techniques of preparing Chinese dishes and are eager to tackle the most elaborate and difficult ones.

Some of the ingredients listed in these recipes may be obtained in partly prepared form in Chinese food stores (for a listing of some of the Chinese stores that will handle mail orders, see pages 39–40). I have also suggested various substitutions to simplify procedures whenever possible. Even so, the preparation of these dishes will require some preplanning and effort. But, if I may quote an old truism, the greater the effort, the greater the reward.

- *BÊCHE-DE-MER (SEA CUCUMBER) WITH CHICKEN AND MEAT BALLS*
  8 SERVINGS

INGREDIENTS

1 cup (after soaking) bêche-de-mer
  (about 2 ounces, dried)
½ cup bamboo shoots, sliced
½ cup boiled chicken breast, in chunks
½ cup ham, in slices 1" x 1" x ¼"
8 meat balls
4 dried mushrooms
12-14 snow peas (about 2 ounces)
1 cup chicken broth
1 teaspoon salt
½ teaspoon sugar
1 teaspoon cornstarch

For meat balls:

6 ounces ground pork
1 teaspoon soy sauce
1 teaspoon dry sherry
¼ teaspoon salt
¼ teaspoon sugar

PREPARATION

Soak and precook bêche-de-mer (see under *Tips*) and cut into ½" pieces.

Soak mushrooms in warm water for 20 minutes. Cut each mushroom into 2 to 4 pieces.

String the snow peas, cut each in half and parboil them. Cool and leave them floating in cold water until ready to use.

Mix 1 teaspoon soy sauce, 1 teaspoon sherry, ¼ teaspoon salt and ¼ teaspoon sugar with the ground pork and make 8 balls. Sear on all sides in a little oil in a small frying pan. When they are firm, remove and set aside. (The pork will not yet be fully cooked.)

Dissolve 1 teaspoon cornstarch in 1 tablespoon cold water.

COOKING PROCEDURES

Bring to boil 1 cup chicken broth and add meat balls, mushrooms and sliced bamboo shoots. Boil for 5 minutes.

Add bêche-de-mer, chicken and ham. Turn flame to medium, cover and cook for another 5 minutes.

Turn flame to high. Thicken mixture with pre-dissolved cornstarch.

Mix in the snow peas. As soon as these are heated through, the dish is ready to serve.

TIPS

Bêche-de-mer are found in the sea. They are like small cucumbers in shape. Dried bêche-de-mer, which is black in color, can be purchased in Chinese food stores (see pages 39–40 for partial listing). They should be soaked in warm water for 24 hours; the water should be changed several times. Then cut the underside and clean out the inside of the bêche-de-mer. Rinse in cold water. Cook for four hours in water over a low flame. The bêche-de-mer will swell to 4 times their original size. The texture will be soft. Pieces of bêche-de-mer are used in soups and in many pork and poultry dishes.

• BIRD'S NEST SOUP
8 SERVINGS

INGREDIENTS

4 tablespoons pre-prepared bird's nest
2 tablespoons diced ham
¼ cup water chestnuts
¼ cup Chinese mushrooms
4 cups chicken broth
1½ teaspoons salt
1 tablespoon cornstarch

PREPARATION

Soak the bird's nest in lukewarm water for 30 minutes. Clean off any foreign substance.

Soak mushrooms in warm water for 20 minutes. Dice mushrooms.

Dice water chestnuts.

Dissolve 1 tablespoon cornstarch in 2 tablespoons water.

COOKING PROCEDURES

Heat 4 cups chicken broth and add bird's nest. Boil over medium flame for 20 minutes.

Add water chestnuts, mushrooms and ham. Cook for 5 minutes.

Add 1½ teaspoons salt and stir a few times.

Thicken with pre-dissolved cornstarch. Serve hot.

TIPS

The bird's nest called for in this recipe is the nest of a species of sea swallow that makes its home high on the coastal cliffs along the China Sea. These swallows build their nests out of various things floating in the sea, mostly an assortment of seaweeds. After years of exposure to the sun, rain and winds, the materials in the nests undergo a chemical change. The Chinese believe that this chemical process lends a tonic value to the nests and that anyone who drinks half a cup of soup made from these nests is assured of good health and long life.

Bird's nest soup is expensive because of the scarcity of nests of the required variety and because of the labor involved in preparing them. Someone has to spend a lot of time separating feathers and down from the edible portion of the nest. Actually, the flavor of the bird's nest soup comes mainly from the chicken broth used in its preparation. Bird's nest in pre-prepared form is sold in Chinese food stores (see pages 39–40 for partial list) and can be kept for years.

- **BUDDHA'S DELIGHT**
  8 SERVINGS

INGREDIENTS

> 20 dried ginkgo nuts
> 16 dried tiger-lily buds (golden needles)
> 14 fresh snow peas
> 6 water chestnuts
> 4 medium-sized dried Chinese mushrooms
> 4 dried lotus roots
> ¼ cup (after soaking) dried tree ears
> ¼ cup bamboo shoots, sliced
> ¼ cup vegetable steaks
> ¼ cup cooked carrots, sliced
> ¼ cup taro or 1 small Irish potato
> 1 tablespoon dried hair-seaweed
> 1 teaspoon soy sauce
> 1 teaspoon salt
> 1 teaspoon sugar
> ¼ teaspoon monosodium glutamate
> ½ teaspoon sesame-seed oil

PREPARATION

Soak the following ingredients in separate bowls, in warm water, for 20 minutes: tiger-lily buds, mushrooms, lotus roots, tree ears, hair-seaweed. Wash and drain.

Crack the ginkgo nuts and shell them. Pour boiling water over nuts and let stand for 5 minutes. Remove the pinkish inner skin.

Parboil the snow peas and let them float in cold water.

Slice the water chestnuts.

Cut the vegetable steak into 1" pieces. Cut lotus roots and mushrooms into similar-sized pieces.

Halve the taro. If Irish potato is used instead of taro, cut into thin slices.

COOKING PROCEDURES

Bring 1 cup water to boil. Add mushrooms, tree ears, tiger-lily buds, lotus roots and ginkgo nuts and continue to boil for 5 minutes.

Add salt, sugar, and soy sauce and mix well.

Add water chestnuts, carrots, bamboo shoots, vegetable steak and hair-seaweed. Mix a few times. Cover and cook over medium flame for 5 to 7 minutes. Add taro or sliced potato. Mix and cook for 2 more minutes.

Add monosodium glutamate and snow peas. Mix thoroughly and cook for 1 minute more. Just before serving, add ½ teaspoon sesame-seed oil. Serve hot or cold.

TIPS

This is a famous vegetarian dish. Buddhists are vegetarians—hence its name. It usually combines 10 to 12 different kinds of vegetables, both fresh and dried. It does take some time to gather together all the necessary ingredients, to soak, clean, cut and drain them. But all this effort is well rewarded in the end.

Ginkgo nuts, tiger-lily buds, lotus roots, fungi (tree ears), hair-seaweed and mushrooms are obtainable from Chinese food stores (see partial listing on pages 39–40). All of these will keep for several months, and can add interest to other dishes.

Taro may be purchased fresh or in cans. Canned taro is much easier to use. It is available in fancy food stores and Japanese food stores.

Vegetable steaks are also sold in cans and can be purchased in health-food stores. Once the can is opened, the steaks should be used within a few days.

• CHICKEN AND CHINESE SAUSAGE RICE
6 SERVINGS

INGREDIENTS

2 cups long-grain rice
2 chicken legs
2 Chinese sausages
1 scallion, cut in 2" pieces
4 dried Chinese mushrooms
2 slices fresh ginger root
1 tablespoon dry sherry
2 tablespoons soy sauce
½ teaspoon salt
½ teaspoon sugar

PREPARATION

Rinse rice under cold water for 2 minutes or until the water runs clear.

Cut chicken, with skin and bones, into 1" pieces, using heavy cleaver.

Marinate for 1 hour in scallion, ginger, 1 tablespoon sherry, 2 tablespoons soy sauce, ½ teaspoon salt and ½ teaspoon sugar.

Slice the sausages into ½"-thick pieces.

Soak mushrooms in warm water for 20 minutes. Cut off stems and discard. Cut each cap into 2 to 4 pieces.

COOKING PROCEDURES

Place rice in a casserole, add 3 cups water and bring to boil. Without covering, let it boil for about 5 minutes or until the water is about 70 per cent absorbed.

Arrange chicken, sausage and mushrooms over the rice. Discarding the scallion and ginger, pour the marinating sauce over the rice

Cover, turn flame to low and let simmer for 20 minutes. Remove from fire.

Without disturbing the rice or uncovering the casserole, allow rice to stand for at least 20 minutes before serving. This will finish cooking the rice. Serve from casserole.

TIPS

Chicken breasts can be used instead of legs. If you wish, discard skin and bones before serving.

If Chinese sausages are not available, they may be omitted, but their special flavor enhances this dish. There are two kinds of Chinese sausage: those that are made of pork alone and those that are made of pork and liver. Either kind may be used, but I personally prefer those with pork only. They can be purchased by the pound from Chinese food stores. Each pound contains 8 to 9 sausages. If stored in the refrigerator they will keep for several months. Chinese sausages are made in the Chinatowns of large cities in the United States and Canada.

• DRIED FISH MAW WITH HAM AND PEAS
8 SERVINGS

INGREDIENTS

2 ounces dried fish maw, deep fried
½ cup frozen peas
¼ cup ham slices, 1" x 1" x ¼"
½ cup bamboo slices, 1" x 1" x ¼"
¼ cup soaked Chinese mushrooms
1 cup chicken broth
1 teaspoon salt
1 teaspoon cornstarch

PREPARATION

Soak the fish maw in hot water for 10 minutes. Wash and rinse in hot water several times to get rid of any excess fat. Gently squeeze out all the water and cut into 1" x 1" x ½" pieces.

Cut the soaked Chinese mushrooms into small pieces, similar in size to the fish maw.

Dissolve 1 teaspoon cornstarch in 1 tablespoon water.

COOKING PROCEDURES

In a saucepan, cook the chicken broth with mushrooms, bamboo shoots and fish maw for 10 minutes.

Add ham and peas and cook for 3 minutes more.

Thicken slightly with pre-dissolved cornstarch. Serve hot.

TIPS

Dried fish maw can be purchased, already deep fried, in Chinese food stores. It will keep for several weeks without becoming rancid. The dish is delicate in taste and does not have a fishy smell.

If fresh peas are used instead of frozen, parboil them first and soak in cold water until you are ready to use them.

- DRIED SCALLOPS WITH RADISH BALLS
6 SERVINGS

INGREDIENTS

6 *dried scallops (about 4 ounces)*
20 *medium-sized radishes*
1 *tablespoon sherry*
½ *teaspoon salt*
1 *tablespoon peanut or corn oil*
1 *teaspoon cornstarch*

PREPARATION

Soak the dried scallops in 1 tablespoon sherry and 1 tablespoon warm water overnight.

Bring to boil 1 cup water with scallops added. Cover and turn flame to low. Simmer for 2 hours, or until the scallops are very tender.

Cut off the tops and roots of the radishes. Boil in 1 cup of water for 15 minutes. Drain. Discard the water.

Dissolve 1 teaspoon cornstarch in 1 tablespoon cold water.

COOKING PROCEDURES

Heat 1 tablespoon oil in a frying pan over high flame, add radishes and stir for a minute.

Add ½ teaspoon salt and mix well.

Add the scallops with the remaining juice and cook, covered, over medium flame for 5 minutes.

Thicken with the pre-dissolved cornstarch. Serve hot.

TIPS

Dried scallops can be obtained in Chinese grocery stores. They will keep in a jar for a long time.

• *GOLD COIN MUSHROOMS*
8 SERVINGS

INGREDIENTS

16 *medium-sized dried Chinese mushrooms*
6 *water chestnuts*
1 *pound fresh uncooked shrimps*
2 *egg whites*
1 *tablespoon dry sherry*
1 *teaspoon cornstarch*
1 *teaspoon salt*
1 *tablespoon flour*

For sauce:
1 *cup chicken broth*
½ *teaspoon salt*
¼ *teaspoon monosodium glutamate*
2 *teaspoons cornstarch*

PREPARATION

Soak the mushrooms in warm water for 20 minutes. Boil them in the same water for 5 minutes. Drain. Cut off the stems and discard.

Shell, devein, wash and drain the shrimps. Mince them and mix with sherry, salt and cornstarch.

Mince water chestnuts and add to the mixture.
Add the unbeaten egg whites; mix thoroughly.

Dust insides of mushroom caps with a little flour and stuff each cap with 1 teaspoon of the shrimp mixture.

Dissolve the 2 teaspoons cornstarch in 1 tablespoon water.

COOKING PROCEDURES

Steam mushrooms on a plate, covered, over boiling water for 20 minutes.

In a small saucepan, heat the chicken broth until it boils. Add ½ teaspoon salt and ¼ teaspoon monosodium glutamate and mix well. Then add the 2 teaspoons pre-dissolved cornstarch and stir until sauce thickens.

Arrange mushrooms on a serving plate and pour the sauce over them. Serve hot.

TIPS

The mushrooms can be partly prepared earlier in the day by steaming for 10 minutes only. When you are ready to serve them, finish steaming, make the sauce and pour over them.

Minced fillet of flounder or sole can be used instead of shrimps. Chopped scallion or parsley may be added to the stuffing to lend color and flavor.

● *HAPPY FAMILY*
8 SERVINGS

INGREDIENTS

8 *pork balls*
8 *shrimp balls*
8 *fish balls* (*see page* 94)
¼ *cup prepared bêche-de-mer* (*see pages* 155-56)
¼ *cup fish maw, sliced* (*see page* 161)
¼ *cup abalone, sliced*
¼ *cup water chestnuts, sliced*

¼ cup (after soaking) Chinese mushrooms,
    sliced
¼ cup bamboo shoots, sliced
¼ cup boiled ham, sliced
¼ cup cooked chicken breast, sliced
10-12 snow peas
1 cup chicken broth
1 teaspoon salt
1 teaspoon cornstarch

For pork balls:
6 ounces ground pork
1 teaspoon soy sauce
1 teaspoon dry sherry
¼ teaspoon salt
¼ teaspoon sugar

For shrimp balls:
8 ounces uncooked shrimps
6 water chestnuts
½ teaspoon salt
¼ teaspoon sugar
2 teaspoons cornstarch
1 cup peanut oil, for frying

PREPARATION

Make pork balls as follows:

Mix pork with 1 teaspoon soy sauce, 1 teaspoon
sherry, ¼ teaspoon salt, ¼ teaspoon sugar. Divide into 8
parts and roll each into a ball. Steam on a plate over boiling water for 15 minutes. Save the juice from the meat
balls for later use.

Make shrimp balls as follows:

Shell, devein, wash and drain the shrimps. Mince
with water chestnuts. Mix with ½ teaspoon salt, ¼ teaspoon sugar and 2 teaspoons cornstarch. Heat 1 cup peanut
oil until an oil thermometer registers 375 degrees. Scoop up
1 teaspoon of shrimp mixture and gently drop it into the
oil, turning it a few times with chopsticks to cook evenly.
When shrimp ball turns pink, remove and drain on paper
towel. Continue to fry, one at a time, until there are 8.
Each shrimp ball takes 3-4 minutes.

Slice the abalone and save the juice for use in
the stock.

Soak Chinese mushrooms in warm water for 20 minutes. Cut each mushroom into 2 to 4 pieces (discard stems).

String snow peas and cut each in half.

COOKING PROCEDURES

In a saucepan, heat stock made with chicken broth, reserved abalone juice and juice from steamed pork balls. Add pork balls, shrimp balls, fish balls, fish maw, bêche-de-mer, bamboo shoots and mushrooms, and cook for 5 minutes.

Add water chestnuts, ham and chicken. Mix well and cook for 2 minutes. Add salt and stir a few times.

Add snow peas and abalone slices and, when mixture comes to a boil, thicken with 1 teaspoon predissolved cornstarch. Serve hot.

TIPS

As many as 8 to 10 varieties of meat, poultry and seafood may be used in making Happy Family. Bamboo shoots, mushrooms and snow peas are used both for color and texture. With a combination of so many delicacies, this dish denotes festivity; therefore it is included in the celebration of any happy occasion, whether it is the birth of the first child (but only the male first-born), a wedding, or even a family reunion.

At this point, most of the items used should not be too unfamiliar, as they have already been used in one or more of the preceding recipes.

In a restaurant, where all the ingredients are readily available, preparing Happy Family is not as complicated and time-consuming as it is at home. The actual cooking time, however, is short, and with organization and practice this dish will not be forbiddingly difficult to make.

Whatever is not consumed immediately can be frozen for future use. Just reheat in a saucepan for a few minutes, and all is ready.

- ## PORK SHREDS AND SZECHUEN PRESERVED KOHLRABI

  8 Servings

Ingredients

1 cup lean pork (about 8 ounces)
½ cup bamboo shoots
¼ cup Szechuen preserved kohlrabi
4 dried Chinese mushrooms
1 teaspoon dry sherry
1 teaspoon soy sauce
1 teaspoon sugar
2 tablespoons peanut or corn oil

Preparation

Cut the pork into shreds 2″ x ¼″ x ¼″.

Cut bamboo shoots into similar-sized shreds.

Soak dried mushrooms in warm water for 20 minutes. Cut off stems, discard these and shred the mushroom caps.

Wash Szechuen kohlrabi in cold water and shred.

Cooking Procedures

Heat 2 tablespoons oil in a frying pan over high flame, add the pork and stir for 3 minutes. Be sure to stir continually until the pork turns white.

Add shredded mushrooms, bamboo shoots and kohlrabi and mix well.

Add 1 teaspoon sherry, 1 teaspoon soy sauce and 1 teaspoon sugar and mix thoroughly.

Add ½ cup cold water and bring to boil. Cover and cook over a medium flame for 5 minutes.

Turn flame to high, stir mixture a few times and cook without cover until most of the juice is absorbed. Serve hot.

TIPS

This dish requires more time to cut than to cook, but it can be prepared beforehand and rewarmed over low flame when needed.

Szechuen preserved kohlrabi is sold in cans in Chinese food stores (see pages 39–40 for partial listing). When you open the can, empty the kohlrabi into a jar and store in the refrigerator. Refrigerated, it will keep for several months.

● SHARK'S FINS WITH CHINESE CABBAGE
8 SERVINGS

INGREDIENTS

2 cups soaked shark's fins
(about 4 ounces, before soaking)
1 whole boiled chicken breast
1 cup Chinese cabbage in 1" pieces
½ cup bamboo shoots, sliced
¼ cup soaked Chinese mushrooms
1 cup chicken broth
1 teaspoon salt
½ teaspoon sugar
1 teaspoon cornstarch

PREPARATION

Soak the dried shark's fins in lukewarm water overnight.

Simmer fins in 2 cups of water over a low flame for about 1 hour.

Rinse the fins several times in cold water. Put them in a bowl of cold water and keep in the refrigerator until you are ready to use them.

Cut the boiled chicken breast (without skin and bones) into 1" pieces.

Wash Chinese cabbage and cut into 1" pieces.

Dissolve 1 teaspoon cornstarch in 1 tablespoon cold water.

COOKING PROCEDURES

In a saucepan heat 1 cup chicken broth with mushrooms and bamboo shoots. Bring to boil.

Add 1 teaspoon salt and ½ teaspoon sugar.

Add shark's fins and bring again to a boil. Cover, turn flame to low and simmer for 5 minutes.

Add pieces of Chinese cabbage and chicken and simmer for 5 more minutes.

Turn flame up to high. When liquid boils again, thicken with pre-dissolved cornstarch. Serve hot.

TIPS

Shark's fins, long considered the "most delicate of all delicacies," take a long time to prepare. Partially prepared shark's fins are available in Chinese food stores (see pages 39–40 for partial listing). These will cut down the preparation time considerably. Dishes made with shark's fins are expensive both because the fins are in short supply and because their preparation is so time-consuming. Nevertheless, it is customary to include them in the most formal and elaborate Chinese banquets. Some Chinese chefs base their whole reputation on the way they cook shark's fins.

Soaked shark's fins can be kept in the refrigerator for several days before using. Dried shark's fins will keep for years.

• *SHRIMPS, SZECHUEN STYLE*
8 SERVINGS

INGREDIENTS

    1 *pound fresh uncooked shrimps*
    2 *tablespoons scallion in ¼" pieces*
    2 *tablespoons minced fresh ginger root*
    2 *cloves crushed garlic*
    1 *tablespoon tomato ketchup*
    1 *tablespoon chili sauce*
    1 *tablespoon dry sherry*
    1 *tablespoon soy sauce*
    1 *teaspoon sugar*
    ½ *teaspoon salt*
    ¼ *teaspoon crushed red pepper*
    2 *tablespoons peanut or corn oil*
    2 *cups peanut oil for deep frying*

PREPARATION

Shell and devein the shrimps. Wash and drain. (If shrimps are large cut each in two.)

Deep fry the shrimps in oil heated to 375 degrees for 2 minutes. Drain on paper towel.

COOKING PROCEDURES

Heat 2 tablespoons oil in a frying pan over a high flame. Add scallion, garlic and ginger and stir until scallions turn dark green, about 2 minutes. Discard garlic.

Add shrimp and stir for another minute.

Add 1 tablespoon sherry, 1 tablespoon soy sauce, 1 teaspoon sugar and ½ teaspoon salt. Stir a few more times.

Then add the red pepper, tomato ketchup and chili sauce. Mix again. Serve hot.

TIPS

Ketchup and chili sauce were introduced into Chinese cooking during this century. The Chinese find that with the addition of these two sauces food still tastes Chinese but even more flavorful.

Most seafood dishes should be cooked at the last minute and served immediately. The advance preparation of this dish, however, can be done well beforehand to save time.

- *SOOCHOW CHIANG*
  (PORK, MUSHROOMS AND BAMBOO SHOOTS)
  8 SERVINGS

INGREDIENTS

1 *cup diced lean pork*
½ *cup diced mushrooms*
½ *cup diced bamboo shoots*
½ *cup diced sweet pepper, red or green, or both*
½ *cup diced vegetable steak or choplets*
2 *tablespoons dried shrimps*

2 *tablespoons dry sherry*
2 *tablespoons sugar*
2 *tablespoons Hoisin sauce*
1 *tablespoon bean sauce*
2 *tablespoons peanut or corn oil*

PREPARATION

Soak the mushrooms in warm water for 20 minutes. Cut off stems, discard, and cut caps into dice.

Soak the dried shrimps in 2 tablespoons sherry for 1 hour.

COOKING PROCEDURES

Heat 2 tablespoons oil in a frying pan over high flame and fry the pork, stirring continually, for about 2 minutes.

Add mushrooms, bamboo shoots, shrimps and vegetable steak. Mix well.

Add ½ cup cold water; bring to boil. Cover and cook over medium flame for 10 minutes.

Add 2 tablespoons sugar, 2 tablespoons Hoisin sauce and 1 tablespoon bean sauce and mix thoroughly. Cook 3 to 4 minutes more.

Add ½ cup of diced sweet pepper, mix and cook for 2 more minutes. Serve.

TIPS

This dish, though tasty, is rather salty, and should be served with rice. It will keep for several days in the refrigerator; it can also be frozen. It may be served either hot or cold.

Vegetable steaks or choplets are sold, canned, in health-food stores. They are also available in the specialty food departments of many large department stores.

Hoisin sauce and bean sauce are sold, canned, in Chinese food stores (see pages 39–40 for partial listing). Once the cans are opened, these sauces should be emptied into jars, covered and stored in the refrigerator, where they will keep for a long time. Besides serving as ingredients in cooking, these sauces also can be used as dips. If the taste seems too strong, add a little sugar and corn oil just before using.

Dried shrimps, though they are products of Louisiana, used to be exported mainly to China. They, too, can be bought in Chinese food stores. These shrimps, in their dried state, will keep for several months if stored in a covered glass jar.

5. CHINESE HORS D'OEUVRES

HORS D'OEUVRES WITH AN ORIENTAL FLAVOR:

Butterfly Shrimps
Chicken in Paper
Chinese Meat Rolls
Crabmeat Cocktail Rolls
Curry Beef Turnovers
Dried Peppered Beef
Drunk Chicken
Five-Spice Smelts
Fried Shrimp Wontons
Pearl Meat Balls

Pickled Celery Cabbage
  Stems
Sesame Seed Ping
Shrimp Balls
Shrimp Toast
Smoked Eggs
Soy Sauce Bean Curd
Spiced Chicken Livers
Spiced Soy Sauce Fish
Spiced Skinless Peanuts
Tea-Steeped Eggs
Two-Toned Steamed Eggs

READY-PREPARED CHINESE FOODS TO SERVE WITH COCKTAILS:

Dried Shrimp Slices
Dried Shrimps in Sherry
Preserved Red Ginger in
  Syrup
Chinese Pickled Onions

Fancy Whole Smoked
  Oysters
Prepared "Top Shell on
  Sticks" in Soy Sauce
Baby Abalone on Sticks
  in Soy Sauce

DIPS AND SPREADS WITH CHINESE INGREDIENTS:

Hoisin Sauce–Sour Cream
  Dip
Hoisin Sauce–Cream
  Cheese Spread

Oyster Sauce–Sour Cream
  Dip
Sesame-Seed Oil and
  Peanut Butter Spread

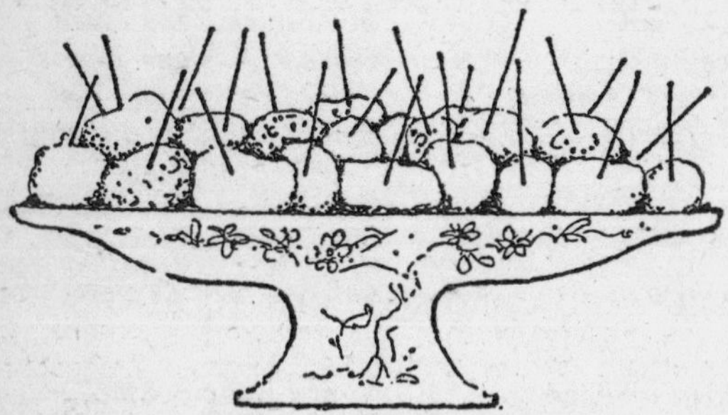

Hors d'Oeuvres with an Oriental Flavor

WHEN I ATTENDED my first cocktail party some years ago, my host was gracious enough to explain this curious American social institution to me. "A cocktail party," he said, "differs from an ordinary drinking party in that we serve hors d'oeuvres at cocktail parties."

This, I thought at that time, was indeed a strange Western custom: serving food to go with drinks. The approach of the Chinese is exactly the opposite. To us, drinks are to complement the food.

The approved manner of drinking Chinese wines (usually rice wines) is not a simple matter of bringing cup to lip. The Chinese will slowly sip warm rice wine while sampling the food set before them. The pace of the alcoholic intake is set by the host, who takes it upon himself to urge his guests to drink for their health, for good luck or for any other reason that might come to mind on the spur of the moment. In return the guests propose toasts to thank the host for his kindness, for his hospitality or for anything at all.

The limited number of excuses for proposing further toasts is no cause for despair. All present may join in traditional finger games, which are usually noisy but not overtaxing—physically. These games are played by two people at a time, who throw out as many fingers of one

175

hand as they wish and simultaneously guess the number of fingers combined. The loser, of course, must pay the penalty. But strangely enough, the penalty is to take still another sip of wine. The host is permitted to drink along with the loser, presumably in the spirit of sympathy.

Chinese hors d'oeuvres may be grouped into two categories: those that are served cold and those that are served hot. The cold dishes are usually on the table before the guests sit down and are intended to be sampled prior to the main courses. The warm tidbits are served at intervals throughout the many-coursed meal.

Strictly speaking, the Chinese do not have any appetizers that fall precisely into the category of cocktail hors d'oeuvres. Some, however, seem particularly appropriate for serving with drinks.

I therefore have included here some of the favorite Chinese appetizers. Many can be prepared beforehand. Most can be reheated, and some can be frozen and kept for future use. These hors d'oeuvres will add a different— let's call it "exotic"—touch to your next party.

- ## BUTTERFLY SHRIMPS
  ### ABOUT 15-18 SHRIMPS

INGREDIENTS

1 *pound uncooked shrimps*
½ *cup flour*
1 *teaspoon baking powder*
½ *teaspoon salt*
¼ *teaspoon monosodium glutamate*
2 *cups vegetable oil for deep frying*

For sauce:
1 *teaspoon Hoisin sauce*
1 *tablespoon chili sauce*
2 *tablespoons tomato ketchup*

PREPARATION

Shell the shrimps but leave the tail portion in shell.

Devein, wash and drain the shrimps.

Make batter by mixing ½ cup flour, 1 teaspoon baking powder, ½ teaspoon salt and ¼ teaspoon monosodium glutamate with ½ cup cold water.

Combine ingredients for sauce.

COOKING PROCEDURES

Heat 2 cups vegetable oil in a saucepan until "waves" form on the surface of the oil (about 375 degrees).

Coat each shrimp with batter, leaving the tail uncoated, and fry, a few at a time, for 3 to 4 minutes.

Serve hot, using sauce for dip.

TIPS

When the tails of the shrimps are not dipped in batter they serve better as holders, and their pink color enhances the appearance of the shrimps. To taste their best, the shrimps should be eaten immediately after cooking.

If you have a small electric saucepan or deep fryer, your guests will enjoy having their shrimps deep fried right at the table; and that way they will surely get them piping hot.

● CHICKEN IN PAPER
MAKES 20 PACKAGES

INGREDIENTS

    1 *large whole uncooked chicken breast*
    2 *or 3 scallions*
    2 *slices fresh ginger root*
    1 *tablespoon dry sherry*
    1 *tablespoon light soy sauce*
    ½ *teaspoon salt*
    ½ *teaspoon sugar*
    20 *squares wax paper, 6″ x 6″*
    2 *cups vegetable oil for deep frying*

PREPARATION

Skin and bone the chicken breast. Cut into 20 slices about 1″ x 1″ x ½″.

Marinate the chicken in 1 tablespoon sherry, 1 tablespoon light soy sauce, ½ teaspoon salt, ½ teaspoon sugar, ginger and scallion for 20 minutes.

Grease the wax-paper squares with a drop of oil, place 1 piece of chicken and a scallion in each, and wrap as shown on opposite page.

Tuck in the flap carefully to complete the envelope.

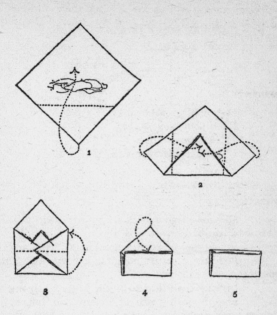

COOKING PROCEDURES

Heat 2 cups of oil to 375 degrees.

Deep fry packages (a few at a time) flap side up for 2 minutes. Turn over and fry a few seconds more. Drain and serve hot. (Please do not eat the paper! Just eat the chicken inside the envelope.)

TIPS

Wax paper is suggested for wrapping because it is the closest thing to the rice paper used in China.

Chicken in Paper is an enticing dish. It is usually served as a course during a banquet. It should be served very hot.

A tasty variation is flank steak, sliced against the grain and cooked the same way as the chicken.

● *CHINESE MEAT ROLLS*
MAKES 20 ROLLS

INGREDIENTS

> ¼ *pound ground pork*
> 1 *teaspoon soy sauce*
> ½ *teaspoon salt*
> 1 *package piecrust mix*

PREPARATION

Mix the ground pork with 1 teaspoon soy sauce and ½ teaspoon salt.

Divide into 20 portions and make 20 oblong rolls.

Pour the piecrust mix into a bowl. Add 3 tablespoons water and mix well.

Divide dough into 20 pieces. Make 20 oblong rolls.

Flatten each piece of dough and roll it large enough to wrap around the pork rolls. Wrap each pork roll in a piece of dough. Pinch edges together firmly.

COOKING PROCEDURES

Heat a *heavy* frying pan (without oil) over a low flame until hot.

Arrange 10 oblong rolls in a row, barely touching one another, in the center of the pan.

When slightly browned on one side, slowly rotate each roll 90 degrees. After turning all 10 rolls, turn 90 degrees more. Repeat this process once more. The whole surface of each roll will now be lightly browned.

Sprinkle 2 tablespoons of cold water over the rolls, cover the pan immediately and cook for 2 to 3 minutes, or until all water is absorbed. Remove from pan.

Repeat the whole process with the 10 remaining rolls. Serve hot or cold.

TIPS

After gradual browning and cooking in covered pan, the pork will be thoroughly cooked. Ground steak may be substituted for pork in filling. These rolls keep fresh for several days in a covered container. In summer, wrap with foil and store in the refrigerator. To serve, reheat rolls in the oven.

● CRABMEAT COCKTAIL ROLLS
MAKES 40 ROLLS

INGREDIENTS

½ cup crabmeat
½ cup ground lean pork
6 water chestnuts
1 tablespoon dry sherry
1 tablespoon soy sauce
1 teaspoon sugar
dash white pepper
2 cups vegetable oil for deep frying
10 sheets egg-roll wrapper, 7" x 7"

PREPARATION

Pick any bits of bone and tendon from crabmeat. Mince the 6 water chestnuts.

Cut 10 egg-roll wrappers into 40 fairly equal triangles.

Preparation of filling

In a frying pan over a high flame, stir fry the pork in 1 tablespoon oil for 3 minutes.

Add 1 tablespoon sherry, 1 tablespoon soy sauce, 1 teaspoon sugar and dash of white pepper and mix well.

Add the minced water chestnuts and crabmeat. Dish and cool thoroughly before using.

Using ½ teaspoon of filling for each roll, wrap as follows:

Place a triangle of dough on board with corner (A) at top of board (Fig. 1). Place filling in center and fold corners B and C toward center until they touch (Fig. 2).

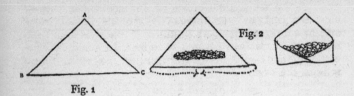

Fig. 1

Fig. 2

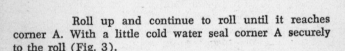

Fig. 3

Roll up and continue to roll until it reaches corner A. With a little cold water seal corner A securely to the roll (Fig. 3).

COOKING PROCEDURES

Heat 2 cups oil to 375 degrees in a saucepan. Deep fry the egg rolls one by one (so they will not stick together) until golden brown. Cut each in half and serve with cocktail picks.

TIPS

Fillings for these rolls can be varied by substituting chopped lobster meat, minced shrimps or ground lean steak for crabmeat.

These cocktail rolls can be prepared in advance and fully deep fried just before serving. Fry rolls lightly at time of making and keep them in the refrigerator overnight or until ready to use. If they are to be frozen, wrap them in foil. Complete the deep frying of the frozen rolls without thawing.

Egg-roll wrappers can be purchased in some Chinese food stores (see pages 39–40 for partial listing).

• CURRY BEEF TURNOVERS
MAKES 24 TURNOVERS

INGREDIENTS

½ *pound ground round steak*
1 *medium-sized onion, chopped fine*
1 *tablespoon soy sauce*
1 *tablespoon peanut or corn oil*
2 *teaspoons curry powder*
½ *teaspoon sugar*
1 *egg yolk, beaten*
1 *package piecrust mix*

PREPARATION

Of filling

Heat 1 tablespoon oil in a frying pan over a high flame and stir fry the steak and onion for about 2 minutes.

Add 1 tablespoon soy sauce and ½ teaspoon sugar and stir a few times.

Add 2 teaspoons curry and mix well. Put into a dish and cool thoroughly before using.

Of turnovers

Empty the piecrust mix into a bowl and add 3 tablespoons of cold water. Mix until smooth. Divide into 24 pieces.

Shape each into an oblong roll 1½" x 2", then flatten each roll.

Using 1 teaspoon curried mixture as filling for each, make half-moon turnovers by folding crosswise.

Brush top with egg yolk.

COOKING PROCEDURES

Preheat oven to 425 degrees and bake turnovers on ungreased cooky sheet for 40 to 45 minutes. When done the turnovers should be lightly browned. Serve hot.

TIPS

Curry Chicken Turnovers can be made by substituting minced chicken breast for ground steak.

Turnovers can be made beforehand and reheated in the oven. If unbaked turnovers are wrapped in foil and kept in the freezer, they will remain fresh for several weeks. When you are ready to use them, bake in the oven according to the above directions.

- DRIED PEPPER BEEF
  UP TO 50 SMALL PIECES

INGREDIENTS

> 1 *pound boneless lean beef*
> 2 *tablespoons peanut or corn oil*
> 2 *slices fresh ginger root*
> 2 *scallions*
> 4 *tablespoons dry sherry*
> 3 *tablespoons sugar*
> 2 *tablespoons soy sauce*
> 1 *teaspoon star anise*
> ½ *teaspoon crushed red pepper*

PREPARATION

Cut beef into 1″ cubes.
Wash scallions and cut into 2″ pieces.

COOKING PROCEDURES

In a saucepan over a high flame heat 2 tablespoons oil and add ginger and scallion. Stir a few times.

Add beef cubes and stir until all are seared.

Add 4 tablespoons sherry, 3 tablespoons sugar, 2 tablespoons soy sauce, 1 teaspoon star anise and ½ teaspoon crushed red pepper in this order. Mix well.

Add 1 cup cold water and bring to boil. Turn flame to medium, cover and cook for 30 minutes.

Turn flame to high; cook (without cover) till all liquid is absorbed. Discard ginger and scallion.

Spread evenly in flameproof dish and allow the beef to cool.

Place beef in warm oven, turn heat off and let dry overnight.

Keep in covered jar until you are ready to use.

TIPS

This is a chewy, flavorful way of cooking beef to be served as hors d'oeuvres. If the beef is dried well it will keep for weeks.

Star anise can be purchased in Chinese food stores (see pages 39–40 for partial listing) or specialty food stores.

The amount of crushed red pepper may be adjusted according to taste, but it is advisable to use at least ¼ teaspoon, and not more than 1 teaspoon, for the quantity of beef given here.

● DRUNK CHICKEN
   MAKES 15 TO 20 PIECES

INGREDIENTS

1 *whole uncooked chicken breast*
1 *slice fresh ginger root*
1 *scallion*
1 *tablespoon salt (3 teaspoons)*
½ *cup dry sherry*

PREPARATION AND COOKING

Wash scallion and cut into 2″ pieces.

Bring 2 to 3 cups of water to a boil in saucepan. Drop in the chicken breast with the scallion, ginger root and 2 teaspoons salt. Bring again to a boil. Continue boiling for 10 minutes. Turn off flame but let the chicken remain soaking in the water for 10 more minutes.

Remove chicken to plate and discard skin and bones while still warm. Sprinkle with 1 teaspoon salt.

Place chicken in a container with cover, add ½ cup sherry, cover and keep overnight in the refrigerator.

When ready to serve, cut chicken into 1″ cubes. Serve cold.

TIPS

This dish is interestingly called "Drunk Chicken" because of its overnight soaking in sherry. It has an intriguing, exotic taste.

● FIVE-SPICE SMELTS
MAKES 15 TO 20 PIECES

INGREDIENTS

1 *pound fresh, whole smelts*
2 *slices ginger*
2 *scallions, cut up*
2 *tablespoons soy sauce*
2 *tablespoons dry sherry*
1 *tablespoon sugar*
1 *teaspoon salt*
1 *teaspoon five-spice powder*
2 *cups vegetable oil for deep frying*

PREPARATION

Cut off heads of smelts. Wash and drain fish. Cut each into 2 or 3 pieces.

Marinate overnight in 2 tablespoons sherry, 2 tablespoons soy sauce, 1 tablespoon sugar, 1 teaspoon salt, 2 slices ginger and 2 scallions.

Just before frying, drain and blot dry.

COOKING PROCEDURES

Heat oil to 375 degrees. Fry smelts, a few at a time, until dark brown. Drain on paper towels.

When all the smelts are fried, sprinkle with 1 teaspoon five-spice powder. Serve immediately if they are to be eaten hot.

TIPS

Five-spice powder (see page 12) can be purchased from Chinese food stores (see pages 39–40 for partial listing). A small amount of this powder goes a long way.

These smelts are good cold as well as hot.

● FRIED SHRIMP WONTONS
MAKES 40 WONTONS

INGREDIENTS

½ *pound uncooked shrimps*
¼ *pound ground pork*
1 *tablespoon dry sherry*
1 *tablespoon soy sauce*
dash white pepper
2 *cups vegetable oil*
10 *sheets wonton wrapper, 7″ x 7″*

PREPARATION

Shell and devein the shrimps. Wash and drain. Mince.

Heat 2 tablespoons oil in a frying pan over a high flame and stir fry the pork for 2 minutes.

Add 1 tablespoon sherry, 1 tablespoon soy sauce, and a dash of white pepper. Mix well.

Add minced shrimps. Stir for another minute.

Put into a dish and cool thoroughly.

Divide each square of wrapper into 4 little squares.

How to wrap wontons:

Put ½ teaspoon of filling just off-center on each 4″ square (Fig. 1). Fold over at the center. Gently press the edges together (Fig 2). Fold in half again lengthwise (Fig. 3). Pull the two corners one over the other and press them together with a little water (Fig. 4). A properly wrapped wonton resembles a nurse's cap (Fig. 5).

COOKING PROCEDURES

Heat 2 cups oil in a saucepan until it reaches 375 degrees. Then deep fry the wontons for 2 minutes, a few at a time. Serve hot.

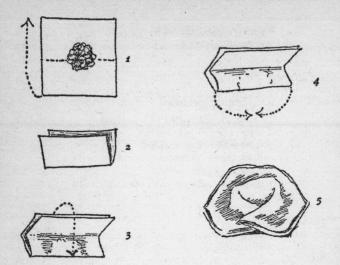

TIPS

Crabmeat and lobster meat can be prepared and used as filling in the same way as shrimps. Wonton wrappers are available in Chinese food stores. For directions on making your own wrappers see pages 52–53.

Wontons may be frozen before frying and kept for several days. When ready to use, thaw and deep fry as above.

In shelling uncooked shrimps, take off all the shell except that near the tail. To shell the tail, press hard on it to break the shell and then pull gently on the shell with the left hand while holding the shrimp in the right. The tail shell will slide off like a glove. Try not to break off the tail itself. The tail is the part that will turn bright pink in frying, adding a lively touch of color to the cooked shrimp.

• PEARL MEAT BALLS
ABOUT 30 BALLS

INGREDIENTS

> 1 *cup glutinous, or sweet, rice*
> 2 *cups ground pork*
> 12 *water chestnuts*
> 1 *egg*
> 1 *tablespoon dry sherry*
> 1 *tablespoon soy sauce*
> 1 *teaspoon salt*
> 1 *teaspoon sugar*

PREPARATION

Mince 12 water chestnuts and mix with pork.

Add 1 tablespoon sherry, 1 tablespoon soy sauce, 1 teaspoon sugar, 1 teaspoon salt and 1 egg to the pork and mix thoroughly.

Soak 1 cup glutinous rice in 2 cups cold water for 30 minutes. Rinse clear and drain. Let stand for about 10 minutes.

Take 1 heaping teaspoonful of meat and roll into a ball. Then roll the ball in the rice until it is all covered with rice.

Repeat this process until all the meat is used up.

COOKING PROCEDURES

Arrange the meat balls on a plate and steam for 1 hour. In arranging, be sure to allow room for the rice to swell as it cooks.

TIPS

If these meat balls are made the day before serving, steam for 45 minutes only. Cool and put in the refrigerator. Before serving, steam again for 20-25 minutes.

Glutinous rice is sold in Chinese food stores (see pages 39–40 for partial listing).

These are called "pearl" meat balls because of the pearly, shining appearance of the rice after steaming.

● PICKLED CELERY CABBAGE STEMS
ABOUT 40 PIECES

INGREDIENTS

1 pound celery-cabbage stems
3 tablespoons salt
1 teaspoon Szechuen peppercorns
1 teaspoon dry sherry
2 dried whole red peppers (optional)
1½ cups warm water

PREPARATION

Wash and drain the celery cabbage. Cut the stems in 2″ x ½″ pieces. Let dry for half a day or overnight.

Dissolve salt in 1½ cups warm water. Add 1 teaspoon peppercorns, 2 red peppers, if used, and sherry. Cool.

Pour seasoned liquid into a jar and add the celery-cabbage stems. Cover and let stand in the refrigerator for 3 days.

Before serving, remove the celery cabbage from liquid and blot dry.

TIPS

The same solution may be used a second time with the same amount of celery cabbage. Add only 1 teaspoon salt the second time.

Carrot sticks, string beans and celery stalks cut into 2″ pieces can be pickled the same way and will be ready in about 4 days.

● SESAME SEED PING
MAKES 20 PINGS

INGREDIENTS

1 roll prepackaged dough, already divided into sections
1 tablespoon minced ham

1 *tablespoon finely chopped scallion*
1 *tablespoon finely chopped leaf lard (optional)*
2 *tablespoons sesame seeds*
1 *egg white*

PREPARATION

Open the roll of prepackaged dough and cut each piece in half. With your fingers, spread each half into a flat, round shape about 2″ in diameter.

In the center of each circle place a bit of ham, scallion and lard. Pinch the edges together into a ball. Flatten slightly.

Dip one side in egg white and then dip the same side in sesame seeds.

With sesame-seed side up, arrange rounds on an ungreased cooky sheet.

COOKING PROCEDURES

Preheat oven to 400 degrees. Bake the pings for 10 to 12 minutes.

TIPS

If other shortening than leaf lard (unrendered lard) is used, ¼ teaspoon to each ping will be about right. These may be served either hot or cold.

• SHRIMP BALLS
MAKES 30 BALLS

INGREDIENTS

1 *pound uncooked shrimps*
6 *water chestnuts*
1 *egg*
1 *teaspoon salt*
½ *teaspoon sugar*
1 *teaspoon cornstarch*
2 *cups vegetable oil*

Preparation

Shell and devein the shrimps. Wash and drain. Mince.

Mince the 6 water chestnuts.

Mix shrimps, egg and water chestnuts with 1 teaspoon salt, ½ teaspoon sugar and 1 teaspoon cornstarch.

Cooking Procedures

Heat 2 cups of oil in a small saucepan until oil "floats like a cloud" (about 375 degrees on oil thermometer).

Scoop 1 generous teaspoon of shrimp mixture and gently drop it into the oil. When shrimp ball turns pink, take it out and put on paper towel to drain.

Repeat process until entire mixture is used up.

Tips

The regular Chinese method for making shrimp balls calls for 1 tablespoon of minced leaf lard (unrendered lard) or regular lard mixed with shrimp to make balls more tender; but, as animal saturated fats are not considered to be particularly good for the health, I have purposely left out the lard, and I find the results quite satisfactory.

Shrimp balls can be made ahead and warmed in the oven before serving. Of course it is always best to serve immediately, as deep-fried food is at its tastiest then.

● SHRIMP TOAST
   Makes 24 Pieces

Ingredients

½ pound uncooked shrimps
4 water chestnuts, finely chopped
1 egg, slightly beaten
6 slices bread, at least 2 days old
1 teaspoon salt
½ teaspoon sugar
1 tablespoon cornstarch
2 cups peanut or corn oil

PREPARATION

Shell and devein the shrimps. Wash and drain. Mince.

Thoroughly mix minced shrimps and chopped water chestnuts with 1 teaspoon salt, ½ teaspoon sugar, 1 tablespoon cornstarch and the beaten egg.

Trim the crust off each slice of bread. Cut each slice into 4 triangles.

Spread 1 teaspoon shrimp mixture over each triangle.

COOKING PROCEDURES

Heat 2 cups of oil in a saucepan to a temperature of 375 degrees. Gently lower the bread into the oil with the shrimp side down. After 1 minute, turn over and fry for a few more seconds. Fry only a few at a time. The triangles should be golden brown when done. Drain on paper towels. Serve immediately.

TIPS

Be sure to use stale bread as it absorbs less oil than fresh bread—and Shrimp Toast should be crisp. Like other deep-fried foods, Shrimp Toast is at its best when served immediately. If necessary, however, it can be made ahead and reheated in the oven to serve. These toast triangles can also be frozen and reheated without thawing.

• *SMOKED EGGS*
MAKES 12 PIECES

INGREDIENTS

6 *eggs*
2 *tablespoons soy sauce*
1 *teaspoon sugar*
1 *teaspoon salt*
1 *teaspoon liquid smoke*
½ *cup water*

PREPARATION

Boil eggs for 5 minutes. Cool completely and shell. Pierce each egg once with a sharp knife.

Heat ½ cup water with 2 tablespoons soy sauce, 1 teaspoon sugar and 1 teaspoon salt.

Place the 6 shelled eggs in a quart jar and pour the warm liquid over them. When the liquid has cooled, place jar in refrigerator and let stand overnight.

Next day add 1 teaspoon liquid smoke and let them stand for at least 2 hours before serving. To serve, cut each egg in half. Serve cold.

TIPS

The 5 minutes of boiling time is counted from the time the water is boiling to the time the flame is turned off. Be sure to start eggs in cold water. Eggs should be brought to room temperature before boiling.

The eggs are pierced so that the flavor of the liquid and liquid smoke will be fully absorbed. Liquid smoke is sold in fancy food stores.

● SOY SAUCE BEAN CURD
MAKES 24 PIECES

INGREDIENTS

    6 *pressed bean curds*
    3 *tablespoons soy sauce*
    1 *tablespoon sugar*
    ½ *teaspoon salt*
    ½ *teaspoon star anise*
    ¼ *teaspoon monosodium glutamate*
    1 *cup cold water*

PREPARATION AND COOKING

To 1 cup water add 3 tablespoons soy sauce, 1 tablespoon sugar, ½ teaspoon salt, ½ teaspoon star anise and ¼ teaspoon monosodium glutamate. Boil for 5 minutes.

Add 6 pressed bean curds. Boil over medium heat for 10 minutes.

Remove from heat. Leave bean curd in liquid for 2 hours. Drain.

Cut into small squares or triangles. Serve cold.

TIPS

Pressed bean curds are made from fresh bean curd. To press, wrap each piece of bean curd in cheesecloth and place between two flat boards. Put a weight on the boards. A large bowl of water or a heavy book can serve as a weight. Increase weight twice at intervals of 10 minutes. After an hour, unwrap the bean curd and it will be ready for cooking.

● *SPICED CHICKEN LIVERS*
MAKES 12 OR MORE SERVINGS

INGREDIENTS

1 *pound chicken livers*
2 *slices fresh ginger root*
1 *scallion*
2 *tablespoons dry sherry*
3 *tablespoons soy sauce*
1 *tablespoon sugar*
1 *teaspoon star anise*
¼ *teaspoon crushed red pepper*

PREPARATION

Wash livers and drain.
Wash scallion and cut into 2" pieces.

COOKING PROCEDURES

Put liver in a quart saucepan with 2 slices ginger root, scallion, 2 tablespoons sherry, 3 tablespoons soy sauce, 1 tablespoon sugar, 1 teaspoon star anise and ¼ teaspoon crushed red pepper, and bring to boil. Mix a few times.

Add ¼ cup cold water and bring to boil again.

Turn flame to medium, cover and cook for 15 minutes. Cool.

Cut or slice the livers and serve cold.

TIPS

Since the livers are served cold, they may be prepared several days ahead. In that case, leave the liver in the sauce to let the flavor soak in.

Chicken gizzards may also be prepared in the same manner. The only difference is in the cooking time. Turn flame to low and let the gizzards simmer for 30 minutes.

● *SPICED SKINLESS PEANUTS*
MAKES 12 OR MORE SERVINGS

INGREDIENTS

3 cups raw skinless peanuts
½ cup coarse salt
½ cup sugar
1 teaspoon wine vinegar
1 teaspoon star anise
4 cups water

PREPARATION

Boil 4 cups water. Add ½ cup salt, ½ cup sugar, 1 teaspoon vinegar and 1 teaspoon star anise.

Stir a few times to make sure that both salt and sugar are completely dissolved. Then add 3 cups peanuts. Bring to boil and boil for 2 minutes.

Turn off flame and let the peanuts remain in the liquid for 5 minutes. Drain and spread the peanuts with the star anise on a large tray overnight to dry.

COOKING PROCEDURES

Roast the peanuts in the oven at 350 degrees for 10 minutes.

Stir the peanuts thoroughly and continue roasting at 250 degrees for 15 minutes more.

Turn off heat but leave peanuts in oven until they are cool.

Store peanuts in jars and use as desired.

TIPS

Raw skinless peanuts can be purchased in Chinese grocery stores and nut stores.

These peanuts, roasted without oil, are less fattening than those with fat added. They will keep, stored in a jar, for weeks.

It may seem that a lot of sugar and salt are called for in this recipe, but notice that the water, with both the sugar and salt, is drained from peanuts after a few minutes.

Roast the star anise along with the peanuts to add flavor.

• SPICED SOY SAUCE FISH
ABOUT 12 PIECES

INGREDIENTS

1 *pound carp*
4 *slices fresh ginger root*
2 *scallions, in 2" pieces*
4 *tablespoons sherry*
3 *tablespoons soy sauce*
1 *tablespoon sugar*
¼ *teaspoon salt*
1 *teaspoon five-spice powder*
2 *cups vegetable oil*

PREPARATION

Wash and clean the carp. Cut into ½″ slices.

Marinate for at least 4 hours in 4 tablespoons sherry, 3 tablespoons soy sauce, 1 tablespoon sugar, ¼ teaspoon salt, ginger root and scallion.

Remove carp from marinade and blot dry, reserving the marinating sauce.

COOKING PROCEDURES

Heat 2 cups of oil to 375 degrees.

Heat the marinating sauce to almost boiling. Lower flame and keep sauce hot.

Deep fry each piece of fish in oil for 2 to 3 minutes, or until golden brown.

Immediately dip each piece of fish in the hot sauce for 5 seconds. Repeat process with all the fish. Spread out on paper towels to drain.

Sprinkle the teaspoon of five-spice powder over fish and serve.

TIPS

The Chinese call this "smoked fish," although usually it is not smoked, but cooked as above. Since the carp slices have both skin and bone, you may, for convenience, substitute fillets of flounder cut into small pieces, marinated and deep-fried. This tastes quite like the carp, but without the skin and bones, and you may find you like it as well.

● *TEA-STEEPED EGGS*
MAKES 12 PIECES

INGREDIENTS

6 *eggs*
2 *tea bags*
1 *tablespoon salt*
1 *teaspoon star anise*

PREPARATION

Hard boil the eggs
Cool and crack the eggs. Do not shell.

COOKING PROCEDURES

Place eggs in a saucepan with just enough water to cover them. Add 1 tablespoon salt and 1 teaspoon star anise. Bring to boil.

Add the 2 tea bags. Turn flame to low and simmer for 1 hour. Turn off flame and leave eggs in liquid overnight.

To serve, shell and slice in half. Serve cold.

TIPS

As there are no tea bags in China, cloth is used to wrap the leaves. Loose tea leaves would stick to the eggs.

When cracking the eggs, care should be taken not to hit the eggs so hard that parts of the shell will fall away. When eggs are properly cracked, the liquid that seeps through etches picturesque lines on the eggs, besides giving them a tea flavor.

● *TWO-TONED STEAMED EGGS*
MAKES 20 TO 24 PIECES

INGREDIENTS

1 *"thousand-year"* egg
3 *fresh eggs*
½ *teaspoon salt*

PREPARATION

Beat the 3 fresh eggs.

Clean and shell the "thousand-year" egg and cut it into small pieces. Mix with beaten egg.

Place mixture in small flameproof dish.

COOKING PROCEDURES

Steam eggs for 10 minutes over high flame. Cool.
Slice into pieces 1″ x ½″ x ¼″.
Serve cold.

TIPS

A "thousand-year" egg is cured in lime for about 6 weeks, not 1,000 years. The egg does, however, take on a grayish color that suggests antiquity. "Thousand-year" eggs are imported from Formosa, and are also prepared in this country. They are sold in Chinese food stores (see pages 39–40).

The combination of fresh eggs and "thousand-year" egg makes this dish colorful and different. It is sure to be a conversation piece at a cocktail party.

Ready-Prepared
Chinese (and Japanese) Foods
to Serve with Cocktails

- ### DRIED SHRIMP SLICES

These are sold in packages of 4 and 8 ounces. Deep fry in hot oil and serve like potato chips.

- ### DRIED SHRIMPS IN SHERRY

Although these dried shrimps are products of Louisiana, they are found primarily in Chinese food stores. To serve: Soak ¼ cup dried shrimps in 2 tablespoons dry sherry for at least 2 hours. Drain off liquid before serving.

- ### PRESERVED RED GINGER IN SYRUP

Slice the ginger and serve with cocktail picks.

- ### CHINESE PICKLED ONIONS

These onions, packed in jars, can be purchased in Chinese food stores. Drain and serve.

● *FANCY WHOLE SMOKED OYSTERS IN COTTONSEED OIL*

These come in cans. Simply open and serve.

● *PREPARED "TOP SHELL ON STICKS" IN SOY SAUCE*

Snails, already cooked, in cans. Open the can, pull out the sticks and serve cold.

● *BABY ABALONE ON STICKS IN SOY SAUCE*

Serve as Top Shell on Sticks.

Dips and Spreads with Chinese Ingredients

- HOISIN SAUCE–SOUR CREAM DIP

Mix the following ingredients:
>   3 *tablespoons sour cream*
>   2 *teaspoons Hoisin sauce*
>   2 *teaspoons chili sauce*
>   2 *teaspoons tomato ketchup*

- OYSTER SAUCE–SOUR CREAM DIP

Mix the following ingredients:
>   4 *tablespoons sour cream*
>   1 *tablespoon oyster sauce*
>   1 *teaspoon sugar*
>   ¼ *teaspoon tabasco sauce*

- HOISIN SAUCE–CREAM CHEESE SPREAD

Mix the following ingredients:
>   2 *ounces cream cheese with chives*
>   1 *teaspoon Hoisin sauce*
>   1 *teaspoon chili sauce*
>   ½ *teaspoon sugar*

- *SESAME-SEED OIL–PEANUT BUTTER SPREAD*

Mix the following ingredients:

    2 *tablespoons peanut butter*
    2 *teaspoons sesame-seed oil*
    1 *square preserved bean curd*
   10 *drops hot sauce*

6. FOUR REGIONAL WAYS OF PREPARING DUCK

Regional Chinese Cooking

CHINA IS A VAST LAND, a little larger in area than the United States. But throughout China's long history it has had neither communications nor a system of transportation to cope with this vastness. The result: the people of the various regions in China have developed their own customs and their own versions of the Chinese language. In fact, the two hundred and fifty-odd dialects of the Chinese language are often so different from one another that a person from one region has the greatest difficulty understanding a person from another region. In such an awkward situation the two can always resort to sending notes back and forth—by some stroke of fortune, the written language has managed to remain uniform for all parts of the country.

Just as the mode of living varies from region to region, so has each region of China developed its own style of cooking. The differences are sharpened by the fact that certain foods are available only in certain regions. Obviously the people living in a coastal region are more apt to eat seafood than those making their homes in an inland area.

For ready identification, the various styles of cooking are often named after the large cities, which regard themselves as the leading exponents of a particular approach to cookery. Thus, the various schools of cooking include such names as Canton, Fukien, Honan, Hunan, Shantung, Szechuen and Yangchow. For the sake of simplicity, suppose we divide China into four roughly equal quadrants—the northeastern, the northwestern, the southwestern and the southeastern—and see how the cooking differs according to geographical location.

Starting with the northeastern region, which includes the Shantung and Honan schools, the distinguishing feature of cooking here is the liberal use of garlic, chives, scallions and leeks. The dishes tend to be light rather than rich. Although the northeastern school of cooking has less variety than that of other regions, the dishes that originated in this section have been widely exported, so to speak, to other sections. The most famous of the northeastern culinary creations is Peking Duck (see page 209). Other typical dishes of this region include Mo-Shu-Ro (page 128), and dishes that, translated literally, have come to be called Sour and Hot Soup (page 138) and Sweet-Sour Fish (page 147).

Moving on to the northwestern region, we come to lands that, generally speaking, are regions of poor soil and severe climate. Because this interior region is far from any seacoast, fresh fish and other seafoods are unobtainable here. Even salt is difficult to obtain in the northwestern region. For this reason, the people often use vinegar—and sometimes lemon—to season their foods. The distinctive taste that results, however, is not widely admired by the people of other sections.

The southwestern region, on the other hand, is a relatively rich agricultural area. In this region developed the well-known Szechuen school of cooking as well as the lesser-known Kweichow and Yünnan schools. The dishes credited to these three schools are characterized by the liberal use of hot peppers and spices. Szechuen Duck (page 211), Szechuen Pork (page 113), Shrimps, Szechuen Style (page 169) and Millionaire Chicken (page 103) are examples of the very hot, peppery, spicy dishes of the southwest.

The region richest in agricultural produce is the southeastern section. What's more, this region boasts the longest coastline, thus providing a variety of seafoods. Fully 90 per cent of all Chinese dishes originated in the Canton, Nanking, Yangchow and other schools of cooking of the southeastern sector. Flank Steak in Oyster Sauce (page 95), Roast Pork (page 119), Lobster with Black Bean Sauce (page 139) and most of the dishes in this book that are prepared by stir frying originated in the southeastern schools of cooking.

Which region in China produces the best cooking? Well, that's a matter of personal preference. The question is apt to be argued—usually loudly—whenever Chinese from different regions get together. The opinions expressed are likely to be based as much on a sense of regional loyalty as on a sense of taste.

In the United States, the majority of the Chinese restaurants follow the Canton school of cooking (except for the chop suey and chow mein dishes which, as I mentioned earlier, can be classified as the "American-Chinese school of cooking"). In recent years, however, a large number of Chinese restaurants that cook in northern style have been established in the larger cities of the eastern coast of the United States. I have often been amused to hear some of my American friends who are well versed in the ways of Chinese restaurants argue among themselves on the virtues and drawbacks of northern versus southern style of Chinese cooking.

Many of the dishes of the various regions of China have been included in previous portions of this book, without any attempt to group them by geographical origin. In this section I have grouped a set of four recipes especially for the purpose of showing students of Chinese cookery the different approaches to cooking in the different regions of China. For our example, we will use duck for all four recipes.

These recipes will give the steps in the preparation of the well-known Peking Duck (with the "doilies" that are served with it); Szechuen Duck (with Lotus Leaf Rolls); Canton Duck; and, least known, but very tasty, Nanking Spiced Duck.

• PEKING DUCK

INGREDIENTS

> 1 *Long Island duckling, 4 to 6 pounds*
> 2 *cups dry sherry*
> 4 *tablespoons Hoisin sauce*
> 2 *tablespoons sugar*
> 10 *to 12 scallions*

PREPARATION

Wash and clean the duck. Hang by the neck for at least 8 hours, preferably overnight, in a cool, airy place.

Place the duck in a rectangular pan just large enough for the bird to lie flat. Pour the 2 cups of sherry over it. Marinate for 1 hour. Turn the duck over and marinate for another hour.

Hang the duck again until there is no dripping.

Wash and clean the scallions. Cut off ½″ above the roots and also discard green tops. The remaining pieces of scallion will be about 4″ in length. Cross-slit both ends about an inch. Soak in ice water for 1 hour. Ends will open up like a flower. Arrange on 2 small plates.

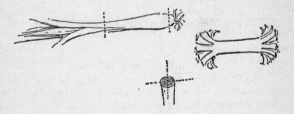

Mix 2 tablespoons sugar with 4 tablespoons Hoisin sauce. Set out on two small plates.

COOKING PROCEDURES

Roast duck for 30 minutes in oven at 375 degrees, 1 hour at 250 degrees, and again for 30 minutes at 400 degrees.

To serve: Slice off skin and cut into pieces 1" x 2". Cut meat into pieces of similar size. Arrange skin and meat on a platter.

To eat: Spread a piece of doily (recipe below) on your plate. Place a piece of meat and a piece of skin in the center. Add 1 scallion and ¼ teaspoon sauce. Roll up the doily and turn over one end. Use fingers to hold roll and eat while still warm.

TIPS

There are many ways to prepare Peking Duck, but I believe that the above recipe is the simplest. In China, Peking Duck is usually prepared in restaurants and has to be ordered at least a day in advance. Shantung restaurants are famous for this method of preparing duck.

The ducks used for this dish in China are fed for many days on special feed so that they will grow fat and tender. But the Long Island ducklings in this country serve the purpose very well.

● *DOILIES FOR PEKING DUCK*

INGREDIENTS

    2 *cups flour*
    1 *cup boiling water*
    2 *tablespoons sesame-seed oil*

PREPARATION

Sift flour and measure 2 cups.

Gradually add boiling water and work with a wooden spoon into a warm dough. Knead gently for 10 minutes and let stand for 10 minutes.

Make into a long roll about 2" in diameter. Cut into ½" pieces and flatten them to ¼" thickness.

Brush a little sesame-seed oil over 1 piece of flattened dough and lay another piece over it. Roll out slowly, from the center out, until the piece is 4" to 5" in diameter. Proceed until all dough is rolled out this way.

Heat ungreased griddle over low flame and heat the dough. When it bubbles slightly, turn over and heat the other side.

While still warm, pull apart and fold at the center with the greased side inside. Repeat until all circles of dough are used up.

COOKING PROCEDURES

Steam for 10 minutes over boiling water before using to wrap duck as described on page 210. Serve hot.

TIPS

These doilies can be made the day before and reheated in a double boiler. The first steaming, however, should be done in a steamer, so that enough vapor will be absorbed to make the doilies soft and easy to use. If no steamer is available use a deep saucepan and set a rack over a deep inverted bowl in this saucepan. Place a piece of cheesecloth over the rack and arrange the doilies on this. Steam, covered, for 10 minutes. Doilies prepared in this way can be frozen, kept for several weeks and resteamed without thawing when you are ready to use them.

• SZECHUEN DUCK

INGREDIENTS

1 *Long Island duckling, 4 to 6 pounds*
4 *slices fresh ginger root*
4 *scallions*
1 *tablespoon Szechuen peppercorns*
2 *tablespoons salt*
1 *quart vegetable oil*

PREPARATION

Wash and clean the duck.

Mince the ginger and chop the scallions. Mix with salt and peppercorns.

Rub the duck thoroughly with this mixture. If there is any left over, put it inside the duck.

Press hard on the breast bone of the duck and break to flatten it. (Duck bones are much more fragile than chicken bones.) Leave in the refrigerator overnight.

COOKING PROCEDURES

Steam the whole duck for about 2 hours. Allow to cool completely.

Heat 1 quart vegetable oil in a large wok or other pan. When oil is heated to about 375 degrees, deep fry the duck for 8 minutes or until golden brown and crisp. Serve whole with Lotus Leaf Rolls (recipe on page 212).

TIPS

To eat, dip in roasted salt and peppercorns. (Roast 2 tablespoons salt and 1 teaspoon peppercorns for 8 minutes in a heavy frying pan on top of the range.)

This duck is so well cooked that a mere push with the chopsticks is sufficient to break the meat off the bones, so knives and forks will not be needed. Pick up a piece of meat and dip into salt-pepper mixture before making a sandwich in the Lotus Leaf Roll. Eat with fingers.

● *LOTUS LEAF ROLLS*

INGREDIENTS

    1 *cup flour*
    ½ *cup milk or water*
    2 *teaspoons sugar*
    2 *teaspoons baking powder*
    2 *tablespoons oil*

PREPARATION

Mix flour with sugar and baking powder.

Gradually add milk and stir with fork or chopsticks to a soft dough. Knead for 5 minutes.

Cover with a clean, dry cloth and let stand for 15 minutes.

After the dough has risen, knead for another 2 minutes.

Make into a roll about 1″ in diameter. Cut into pieces 1″ thick.

Brush with a little oil and fold over. Use fork to make slight indentations all around the edge.

COOKING PROCEDURES

Steam over high flame for 8 minutes. Serve warm with Szechuen Duck.

TIPS

These rolls can be made the day before and re-steamed for 5 minutes before using.

●   *CANTON ROAST DUCK*

INGREDIENTS

1 *Long Island duckling, 4 to 6 pounds*
1 *teaspoon minced garlic*
1 *tablespoon chopped scallion*
1 *tablespoon crushed Chinese parsley*
1 *tablespoon chopped onion*
1 *teaspoon star anise*
1 *teaspoon Szechuen peppercorns*
2 *tablespoons dry sherry*
2 *tablespoons soy sauce*
1 *teaspoon sugar*
1 *tablespoon peanut or corn oil*
4 *tablespoons honey*
2 *tablespoons salt*
1 *teaspoon cornstarch*
1 *tablespoon wine vinegar*

PREPARATION

Wash and clean the duck. Wipe dry both inside and outside.

Tie the duck at the neck with a string so that later no liquid can run through. Hang up by neck for 1 hour to dry.

Rub 2 tablespoons salt over and inside duck.

Stir fry the garlic, scallion, onion, Chinese parsley, star anise and peppercorns in 1 tablespoon oil.

Add 2 cups of water to mixture and bring to boil. Let boil for 5 minutes.

Add 2 tablespoons sherry, 2 tablespoons soy sauce and 1 teaspoon sugar. Mix well.

Pour this sauce into the duck, carefully sew the end and use skewers to fasten it securely, so that no sauce can run out.

Dissolve 4 tablespoons of honey in 2 cups of boiling water. Add 1 tablespoon wine vinegar.

Cooking Procedures

Preheat the oven to 400 degrees. Place duck breast up on rack and roast for 20 minutes. Baste with honey-water-vinegar mixture.

Continue roasting at 350 degrees for 1 hour, basting every 20 minutes.

Reduce heat to 300 degrees and roast for another 30 minutes.

Cool duck slightly. Remove strings and skewers. Drain sauce into a bowl to be served with the duck as it is, or thicken slightly with pre-dissolved cornstarch for gravy.

Carve duck and serve.

Tips

This method of roasting duck is a specialty of the Cantonese. When you go to the food markets in Chinatown, you will see roasted ducks, head and all, hanging by the neck. The sauce has already been drained off. You may buy this duck by the pound, as much or as little as you need. Usually Chinese parsley is served as garnish.

Even in China, Cantonese-style duck is usually prepared professionally. Chinese food stores have special stoves to roast duck, chicken, goose, squab, pork, and even a whole pig. Most Chinese stoves do not have an oven; too much fuel would be required. Thus, roasting is not a common method of cooking in Chinese homes.

• NANKING SPICED DUCK

Ingredients

1 Long Island duckling, 4 to 6 pounds
½ cup coarse salt
2 teaspoons Szechuen peppercorns

PREPARATION

Wash and clean the duck.

Roast the coarse salt with 2 teaspoons peppercorns in a heavy frying pan on top of the stove for 10 minutes.

When salt is cool enough to handle, rub duck with it thoroughly, outside and inside. Wrap duck in foil and store in the refrigerator for 3 to 5 days.

COOKING PROCEDURES

Bring to boil 4 quarts of water in a large pot.

Remove foil from duck and submerge the whole duck in the water. Bring to boil again and boil for 30 minutes.

Cool in the water for 15 minutes. Drain. Cut into small pieces and serve.

TIPS

If desired, save 2 teaspoons of the roasted salt to be used as a dip when serving duck. This duck is very tender and not at all greasy. Bite-sized pieces, without skin and bones, may be used as hors d'oeuvres.

Index

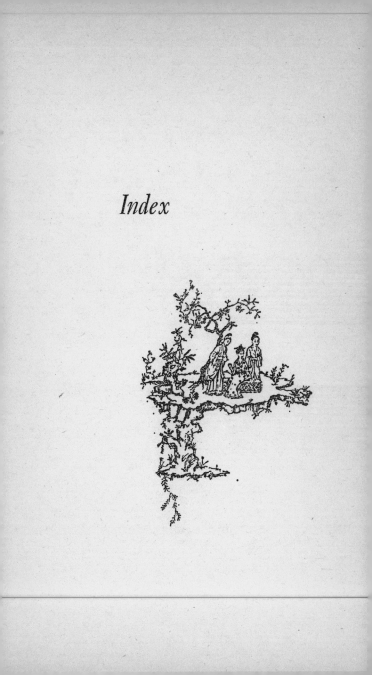

219